to the love that never stops. to t

to the love that knows no limits. to the love without a name or face. to the ones who dare to be weird, strange, and unforgettable. to the ones who dream without ever knowing the ways of how to make it real. keep pushing yourselves and never give up on the fight to become more than who they think you are now. never listen to people who cannot hear the wind and taste the rain. you are not alone in this world and were created to rise from the places you have fallen. i am no saint, but i know a few sinners who are. they have saved me and filled my lungs with air when so many people who i thought loved me, left me there to survive on my own. this is for everyone in my life, and to the ones i haven't met yet, one day we will have the best conversations about nothing at all, which will mean everything to us.

to my moon and muse, thank you, sweet one.

-z.k.d

A Journal From

The Sea

Vol. 2

By: Zachry K. Douglas

a day will come when
someone i have yet to
meet will pick up this
book and after the
last page, they will be
able to feel you holding
them and know the
sound of your voice.

☾

the only way she knew how to live was
by destroying everything she once loved.
she didn't have intentions on breaking what
was in her life before the change happened,
before the clarity in her voice, and the backbone
holding her up was no longer a codependent
structure. the same can be said for the ones who
confused her with a girl they thought was afraid
of the dark, only to be the ones left looking for
the light when she left. we don't intentionally
become who we are. for the most part, it's by
accident and when it happens, we learn how
to evolve. sometimes you need to demolish
yourself in order to find the parts that survived

☾

to know where you were once weak so you
can grow from the rubble of who you used to
be. learn how to add onto the new set of eyes
you picked from flowers nobody cared to look
at because their colors weren't bright enough
and their wilted petals were only good enough
to be kissed by the wind. it takes one person to
believe in a sort of magic that heals all things
dead, but still breathing. it was a lesson
taught to her while pretending to be okay.
she has a bouquet of reasons why she smiles,
and if no one else agrees with her, it's not up for
discussion. she's tired of talking to those behind
a glass wall, worried about being infected by
another human's heart. she's in dire need
of a love that doesn't ask questions.
she's after a love that loves, because of
love itself.

☾

life is funny in that we are always present, but somewhere different even when we don't intend to be. human nature tells us to always give ourselves to the surrounding environment and the places you either visit, or fall in love with. i believe i am still in some of those locations as i take a sip from the sun and chase it down with the rain on days i find my depression gnawing at my ankles. it's a reminder for me to immerse myself in the people i don't know so i can be better at learning who i am. the absolute worst thing anyone can grow into is, is a stranger to

☾

themselves. never forget who you are and always be in present form. it's difficult enough trying to pinpoint your soul on a map you have burned countless times for others to find their way. i think in life you're allowed to be that, but not at the cost of losing yourself in the process. love is too sincere to be mistreated by someone who only knows how to take and never replant what they took. be alert, but don't be timid when love is what you seek. chances are, it has been searching for you longer than you care to know.

☾

some days i wonder how much

of me i really am and how much

i am of someone else's feelings.

☾

you are significant to my growth as a man and if no one else is bold enough to tell you, you matter. you can sit quietly and be the beating heart for the universe, or speak and be the sounding board for those without a voice. you can and you will, because there's something magnificent about simplicity that brings out your very best. you are a moment standing still when everything seems to rush past me, and i don't think i have ever properly thanked you for that. you seem yo have a knack for strange things others would never be captivated by. you are an unscripted apology that stays out with the stars. your tribe is calling again and she is who they are without a doubt. it takes a human a little longer to adjust their eyes when the darkness has been their home. thank you for taking away the demons and invading my heart. my peace has never felt so quiet and calm.

☾

and that was the thing about her, she was
always in pain, but needed someone she
trusted to break down in front of. she was
looking for a comforting shoulder to rest
the madness on for a while. it wasn't in her
character to be as vulnerable as the ones
around her, but she knew it was time to crack
open the shell she had been living in. her power
was being as soft as the wind, while holding
back the hurricane in her soul. the memory she'll
leave you with is a slow burn that escalates into
a wildfire if you have a tendency to regret letting
go of people you love. that's the way she works.
she has a methodical and precise intention of
protecting herself from ignorant and childlike
men who think running with wolves is easy.
just because you can howl, doesn't mean
you can bite, and she's a maven at both.
she's a force you never saw coming;
a rogue wave made from the moon.

she is a small island with an open heart,
softly meditating on love from the wonders
she fills her eyes with. one part miracle and
two parts wild, she cares for the sea inside
of her which is nursing her bones back to
the stability they had lost while being mixed
up with some boy who she can't remember
now. lost in thought, her idea of a life now
consists of figuring out when it's okay to
laugh and whether to cry at the same time.
purging the system of all things negative,
she's a recluse anticipating the next move
until she feels it's time to let someone love
her again. just as the tree lets go of the dead,
we must learn from life in all its intricate ways
of teaching us how to do the same with people
who no longer have the privilege of being in
ours.

☾

love is what we are born with.

fear is what we learn from loving

the wrong person we swear is right

for us. don't murder your heart for

those afraid of bleeding for you.

☾

something important she teaches me every day is that you don't have to understand life in order to hold someone's hand. she looked at me as if the rains were going to wash her away. "sometimes i will just need to, and when i reach for it, don't ask why." that's life in the simplest of forms. respect her wishes and treat her as water and let her save you. if you find a woman like that, be willing to do anything for them. even if they ask you to go outside and just look up for a while, if they want you to go spend time with their soul, never say no. not everyone

☾

will get a chance to know it like you do.
don't waste time thinking about it when you are capable of holding them. we will all need to be held at the most random of times, except there's nothing random about timing. it's the universe's clock and you'll never know if you are the minute hand or the hour hand. all you have to do is enjoy those seconds in-between a passing breath. let love be, or release it free. there are no other options when it comes to the rest of your life.

☾

today is a day i honestly believed i would never be able to see. it has been a struggle and i am still fighting each day for more of what i feel i need. another year older and i am so grateful for each of you who have decided to follow me and my writings. they are a success because of people like you. and i know others will say that your success is only determined by how and what you do and how much you love what you're doing, but i can wholeheartedly say i am in love with art and my passion is writing until i have no more breaths to give. it is my birthday today, but it is a celebration of

☾

something so much more. love and light to you all and thank you again for all of the messages, comments, and support. keep being yourself, even if people don't agree with it. those people can and will always have a back row view of your success. let the light hit you wherever you stand. not everyone will like you or what you do,
but they cannot even fathom what's inside of you. live, laugh, and love when you can, while you can. it's a gift many didn't wake up to open today.

☾

someday you'll have a beautiful life

even though i know right now you

don't think it's possible. we all get

to where we are going. some just

choose to believe in it, while others

are sinking in the same spot they

were told would never give way.

☾

when she cries for the flowers, they rise again. do not bury them with guilt. shower them with hope. life creates rainstorms inside of us that can drown the very essence of who we are if we allow it. now, instead of washing away her present-self, she saves her future by not accepting liars and cowards to drink from her energy. everything lives within the flesh we carry around. do not let it perish for someone who doesn't apply the same effort for your growth.

☾

i hope someone walks into your life, and you finally feel the love you deserve. the love you have always been lending out to people and asking nothing in return.
i hope someone walks into your life and makes you never have to question why. i hope you meet them there and once and for all come to terms with the fact you have always been better than what you've been receiving.
it only takes one person who wants the best for you to realize you have always been good enough. i hope you know how it feels, because once you do, you won't ever settle again for anything less than what makes you feel beautiful, loved, and appreciated.

☾

and if you should ever find yourself giving up on any dream or yourself, please, i beg you, do not. for your soul was made to be dug and is too deep to stop digging now. you're merely skimming the surface of the defining purpose beneath it. there's more to you than ocean waters could ever dream of filling. use the tools you were given: your hands, eyes, feet, heart, and mind. use them until they are bleeding with love. once you find what you're looking for, you will never again be yourself, and to me that's key. we are always in need of growth, and once you stop, that's when you should be afraid,
not before. we encounter too many parasites along the way who try and drain us of what we have uncovered to simply be at rest with the first version of ourselves. dare to push back the blinds so you can actually see yourself in true bloom.

☾

i'm not even sure if i've ever opened my eyes since birth. sometimes it feels as if the sun is too bright to be dying and the oceans are too vast to not have mermaids living in them. babies are crying and trees give birth to ideas all around us. an imaginary world exists, and it is powerful, so i'm going to keep moving until the earth stuck to my feet no longer needs to be washed off. immense possibilities are nesting in my eyes and the sky tends to sway with me as i stumble back to my knees after being gone from my body for too long. i can get lost with the best of them, and hope the angels find them first.

☾

i've discovered other people's demons and made friends with them. they're genuine, but get misconstrued for being evil when they are cowering in the shadows; afraid of the humans acting as saints. i'm not even sure if i've known my eyes before, but i know they have seen the naked light within you; dancing to every particle and atom of love you've kept hidden from those expecting to witness a miracle. we tend to only show ourselves to those who find eye contact to be sexy.

☾

never stop unearthing the smile they tried to bury. the ones who thought you weren't good enough for them. the ones who couldn't stand you looking at anyone but them. the ones who were too busy loving themselves, they forgot you were breathing. the ones who said they would call, but never did, and blamed it on work when it was the weekend. the ones who told you they would always be there for you, then walked out because they were late for someone else. the ones who gave you dead flowers because everything they touched withered and decayed. the ones who thought love was a card game and bluffed at every move to see your reaction. the ones still around, but at

☾

a distance just to stop by and say hello whenever they want to try and ruin your day. the ones who left you in misery and told you it loves company. do not, i repeat, do not allow them to bury you. don't ever think you can change them. chances are they will turn you against yourself and everyone you love. you'll know these people when you see them. they will be wearing a two dollar smile and so full of themselves they won't even remember a goddamn thing about you until it's over. people never forget rarity. be that and love yourself completely first and foremost. you should be your biggest fan, not your own demise.

☾

when you love,

be wild with it.

don't be shy to

walk out of your

own skin.

☾

give me an all out war kind of love.
where souls are battling to get closer
to every moan. give me your nails digging
into my bones and anchoring yourself into
me. do not let go until your arms become
feathers and cannot hold on anymore.
give me your back and turnover kind of love.
from behind with one hand locked in your hair
and the other on your shoulder; gripping it
harder as i go. give me an all out war kind love.
after we are done, i'll bring you to my chest and
love on you gently, kissing your shoulders and
tasting the love left on your lips from our battle.
rough is just a word most are unfamiliar with.
sensual is a place only a few can go. we take
pleasure experiencing both to feed the hunger
we have when we are starving after the first
time.

☾

at night, she lays in her bed with thoughts of another life, but no way of making it happen. it's torture, but she does it so she has something to continually fight for each day. she not only survives the night, she becomes more in love with herself each morning her soul awakes. life is about loving yourself when all things seem impossible, only to figure out how much fight you have in your wings. it started today when she opened her eyes and kicked life square in its face. a face that has laughed and made it almost unbearable for her in the past. she's ready to take it outside of the ring if she must. war paint, bare knuckled and all, she's not scared to get dirty. there's something fierce about this boundless woman that has everyone else rethinking their claims. maybe it takes another mad hatter to know another, but she's crazy in all the right ways.

☾

from my

bones to yours,

allow them

to bloom together.

☾

and then she finally became
more than just another name.

she had become a beating heart,
running through the open flames
of this world.

unafraid of feeling emotions for the
first time, she leaped into uncertainty
with both of her hands free.

you can see her now, drawing in the
clouds and making a life that's fit for
an angel, with wings made of sin.

☾

i will spend my last days
waiting to kiss you once
more. i know i do not
have much time left,
so the precious breaths
i take, i will save them
for you and only you.
as the last words fall
slowly from my lips,
they'll sink into your
beating heart and find
a place where we will
never be apart.

☾

she was ambitious in such a powerful way.
she could sing the angels to sleep with a
tender lullaby and fight off the devil with
the stone that had once imprisoned her
ardent heart.

a human, with a superhuman kind of
passion for life.

☾

i was perfectly lost in thought from the dream i was just in, when her wandering fingers found my skin and brought another soul-rise to my life.

as my heart began to sing her name, i noticed we had created our own horizon. one of which we painted while kissing the places that had yet to be seen by the eyes before us.

☾

and then your name fell graciously from my tongue. as if you had been perched there with your feet dangling from the edge of my lips, waiting for me to speak of you.

(

and when i saw her, i was born again.
it felt like i was as innocent as the day
my opening eyes first saw the glorious
sun, and the night my virgin lips tasted
the water of love raining down around
me; a monsoon of purity

☾

you are so much more than a first and last name. you are made up of more than just skin and bones. you are a beautiful soul with a smile that can change the world. today is so much more than any problems we might face.

it is an opportunity to exchange the pain for a chance to feel the warm embrace from someone who actually cares.

wherever you might be, close your eyes and tell yourself,

"i am free of the binding words they try to throw at me. i am more than alive, because i am finally living my life."

now breathe in and out with me. i am here for you and i always will be.

☾

whatever happens to you and i from this point
forward, i just want you to find the happiness
you need. not because i wrote this telling you
to do so, but because you fucking deserve it.
you are an absolute dream i would die in,
just to experience what being alive with
you feels like; every time i open my
weather-beaten, solitary eyes.

☾

we were walking home from our second date
on a beautiful sunday evening and i noticed
the street lamp i used to pass when i was
younger. i was told it made wishes and dreams
come true. i never thought much about it until
we were directly under it. for some reason she
asked me, "tell me something i don't know
about you." with the snow starting to fall
around us, i felt this electricity run through
my bones and into my soul. i suddenly
reached for her hands and held them as tight
as i could so she could experience it with me.
then i looked at her as if she was the only thing

i would ever need to see again in my life and said, "i love you." the street lamp began to flicker and i could see her face with each strobe of light, as it was interchanging places with my heart; starting and stopping again. all i could make out was the combination of the snow and her face, as they were creating a smile for me to see. i guess dreams and wishes really do come true, when you find the time to believe in them yourself, as much as they believe in you.

☾

and then i saw her.

it was then that i knew the universe never makes a mistake. at a time in my life where i needed hope, she gave me strength and allowed me to believe in myself again. she is the reason the flowers have such bright and beautiful colors. she is not mine, but she is the world in which i live in.

☾

at times i love you is not enough.
i don't want to spend my life
counting seconds, minutes, hours,
or days. i want to count how many
times my hands have touched you
in all of the intricate ways they can
find. i want to count the times i tell
you just how damn beautiful you are
so i can make sure i've said it enough
for the day. i want to live this life with
you, and in the end, i want you to have
my last breath; filled with every "i love
you" i have ever said to you. i need a
love so fierce that it will set fire to the
stars and create a new horizon for the
world to see. love is so much more
than a four-letter word. it is you,
and my soul tells me that every day.

☾

she has faith, but not in a god. she has it deep within her soul for herself. she knew whatever happened in her life, that alone would take her places her weary feet were too scared to travel. her adventures were made by being half-wanderlust and half-mermaid; needing the land, but always making time for the sea.her faith was surrounded by the company of angels and devils she kept in her pockets. for she knew it would take both entities to live a life full of substance, meaning, and mistakes. she was anything but perfect, but she fucking lived for happiness and independence from anything or anyone trying to hold her back from creating her own world of reason.

☾

after we make love, you use my chest as
a pillow and i play with your hair and kiss
your forehead. as my arms are wrapped
around your naked body, i look into your
eyes and tell you, i love you. this moment
is where we live every day we wake up.
it's ours and everything about it makes me
want more of you every second i hold you
firmly against my heart.

there we were, two naked hearts
dancing along the railroad tracks
of life.

listening to the passing cars to
provide temporary music for
our wandering minds.

vibrantly wild and innocent,
our feet never stopped
moving.

☾

i have days where my mind is as quiet as the 18th green at augusta; waiting for the ball to fall directly into the cup.

then there are days where my mind is as loud as a pearl jam concert, but i am the only one there, and the instruments are plugged into my soul; playing with the volume at maximum level.

both are fine with me. i just hope there isn't a happy medium i am missing out on.

☾

i know i could do "this" by myself,
and when i say "this" i mean live,
breathe, dream, and wander.

but i am going to need you,
darling, in order to feverishly
love all of the things i just
listed above.

☾

she told me, "let go," and so i did.
i released every haunting doubt
and inescapable fear that had
ever been birthed inside my
winsome soul.

now i hold onto her heart as if it
was her hand whenever i need to
feel at home.

☾

it should never be about "giving up" things to be with someone. if you love them, you will do whatever it takes to provide a better life for the both of you. therefore, it's a choice and i will always choose us over anything else, every single time.

☾

our love was like the high school
infatuation of our former lives.

where you couldn't wait to get a
homemade book-cover. where we
both wrote the names of each other,
surrounded by paper hearts; showing
it off to the entire school to let them
know who we loved.

for we were and will forever be old
souls filled with young love for one
another.

(

i love her.

not because of who she is or how absolutely beautiful her heart is, but my soul has seen her at both the worst and best times before. i love the fact how when she smiles, my bones grow stronger, allowing me to stand up taller in order to provide the loving space she needs when the world around us tries to cage what we have. we were not born for rules. we were born to be the fire raging in the sky when everything else turns dark and fades away. we love our controlled chaos. it's what separates us from being normal.

☾

i know i cannot give you
everything you might need
right now, but i can provide
you with a loving heart that
sings your name every time
it beats for you and a soul
that will always call you
beautiful. even when you
don't feel as if you are.

if you should go before
i do, i hope my time
here is cut short.

for my purpose lives
and dies with you.

☾

when i get tired, i think of you.
when life tries to get the best
of me, i know the best of us
can conquer anything.

our souls were made to withstand
even the darkest of days, and to be
honest, that's how i found you in the
first place.

☾

now close your eyes with me and feel my arms wrap around you. as i bring you in closer, we start to breathe as one and i tell you, "i am here for you and when my life gets to be wearisome, i rub the bracelet you gave to me with my finger and thumb as a reminder that you are here with me as well." i know these are merely words on piece of paper, but they are from me, to you, in hopes they can bring you the peace you need to get through today. i feel you around me as i am typing this and it brings such steady waves filled with the calm and relaxing sensation you always provide me with. it is a feeling unlike the stars could ever wish of receiving.

☾

you, my love, give my heart the
constant rhythm it needs in order
to give to you the same thing you
have always given to me;

an unshakable belief
that everything is
possible.

my arms will never leave you
and let these words be the
reminder.

☾

i never knew what love was until i met you. the way people had described it to me, i thought i had an idea or maybe felt it before. i guess we all feel and react to love differently. that's the beauty of life in a way; everyone gets to experience it for themselves at one point or another, and then the soul and heart decide if they can agree on what they find. i can honestly tell you it is something that can cure any heartache and soul-ridden pain if it is treated by the right pair of loving hands. be patient and always keep your mind open to the possibility that it might someday find you.

☾

there's a secret place we go when being lost
is the only direction needed and being alive
means dying a hundred times just to feel her
hands locked with mine. in this safe haven,
the only goddamn thing i know is, we speak
the language of our dreams. words are written
on the walls of where we make love and rooms
are filled with every echo of our screams for
each other; constantly begging for more.
people used to tell me that you need to
understand yourself before knowing what
it takes to survive. i look at those same people
now and point to you, and it is then they fucking
realize that sometimes, love from another is
enough to know who you are and more than
enough to live this beautiful and chaotic life.

☾

there is nothing better
than being connected
to someone who values
touch and understands
how to hold you with
their eyes during a
moment that is
captured
in-between
a shared
breath.

☾

with my arms never letting
go of her throughout the
night, she wakes me up
with her lips on mine.

i swear there is nothing in
this world that beats the
taste of her love in
the morning.

as the world transformed around

us, the heart and soul in me

found their way to you;

as they floated in a gravity

made from a love created

by my moon.

☾

once i heard your voice on the other end of the phone, every goodbye my soul had ever felt finally made sense to me. to begin again means parts of your life will end before you believe it to be for the better.
we all experience this journey at different speeds, and it is within those moments of clarity we will encounter a reality we never thought we would see. eventually, time will force our final breath even when we think there is more to give.
and in those last few moments, i know mine will be used to tell you, i love you, and i'll never stop believing in us.

(

we all describe love in our own way and
we will all have a different definition for it.
but to me, every time the sun rises and
sets in my heart, you are love. your body
is my soul's alarm to awake each day with
a smile and your arms are the blanket it
needs to allow me to sleep through the
night.

my definition. my understanding. my reason.

☾

her presence alone is fierce.

it makes the coldest of hearts

catch fire and allows abandoned

souls to believe in humans again.

☾

i'm different i guess, but i choose to stay and be as happy as possible no matter what is happening around my life. at the end of the day, only two things matter to me: is the person i'm with as happy as i am, and if not, how can i make them be. i love you and with that comes the kind of love i have for you.it's the kind that will always be shown either by my lips, hands, words, or the actions they display when they all come together to hold you just right. whether it is 2am or 11pm, all of me speaks of you the

☾

same. every part of me chooses every part of you. when i go to sleep, i will always hold you close to me. i will be protecting you from anything or any dream that may try to worry you. and if you need to wake me, never hesitate to do so. what i am trying to say is, i will never leave you. i am here and this is where i have always needed to be; a place where fingertips are the key that unlocks the growing home inside of you and i.

☾

she is the space in-between

the stars i want to explore.

now you know that even the

rarest form of beauty still

thrives without having to

be seen.

i love her butterfly
soul for the way she
can fully be herself
with and around
me.

it's the way she
roams through my
heart and kisses
every beat she
gives to me that
allows this man the
gift of being alive.

to be special, rare, and strong all at the same time, takes someone who has walked over the moon for others and has been through fires that nobody knows about. this is you, sweetheart. you are more than just fearless. you believe in yourself and that is the most powerful weapon anyone can have. i love you for who you are and how you give these pages of mine words that continue to help and heal an old soul who has been through hell and wondered if there was an actual world above me.

now i know there is.

☾

today, i was trying to understand myself better on my own and i realized just how frustrating it is when you are attempting it that way. it is a group effort with the one you love. no matter how hard it gets, communication will always connect the points and give you the peace you need. whatever the subject is, however it is talked about, it takes you and the other part of your life to come to a realization that everything is better when there is a line that both can call from. an open-hearted discussion will always prevail in the end. so i put my head on her chest and finally relaxed, knowing she was not only helping me, but together, we were growing in life.

☾

waking up next to you,
i will always have more
than i ever dreamed of.
it is in the early hours of
the morning when my
eyes locate your hands
that i truly witness how
powerful a single second
of being with you can be.

and within that second,
i see love laugh and
smile at me.

☾

it was in you that i found
everything i had been
missing and needing;

a heart, soul, and bones to grow old with.

☾

the most honest answer i can tell you as to why i am this way now, revolves around who she is. my life has changed and when that happens, you notice the details which were not there before. the way i sleep, eat, dream, and live my life have all come under construction. i always thought i would be alone in the process of building again. today, i have someone who is not afraid of getting their hands dirty.

☾

the beautiful scars on her soul, shined like the

most brilliant and breathtaking stars in the sky.

all she needs now is someone that finally gives

a damn and is willing to not only discover them,

but notice the smile behind her tears as well.

maybe it's not love. maybe it's something even stronger than the force of that unnamed hurricane. all i know is, i look forward to it each day i'm with you. you have to understand how long it's been since i've held someone the way my arms and thoughts allow me to hold you. life is, and will always be better with you, because i've been learning how to let go of the wrong people in order to know what my heart needed to hold all along.

☾

i've never been the type of person to sleep in late. i love waking up early to enjoy the warming rays of the sun. you may think i am crazy or mad, but i have discussions with myself during the quiet hours of a new day. there is a very raw and emotional feeling i get when it's just me, the whistling birds, the whispering wind, and the calm waters of the ocean. they bring out the very best in me, like you are doing now. my life has always been chaotic and disturbing to a certain degree, and i enjoy our moments unlike anything i've ever done before. for you calm the wild in my soul, allowing me to take in your words and feelings in order to visualize what life could be like when i wake up and i am not alone anymore.

☾

maybe there's a chance that i don't believe in love anymore. maybe i believe we all have a predetermined path and outcome for the choices we've made or for the times we never had the guts to grab life by the throat and live for us. all of this might seem like a late night rambling session, but i know my heart pumps the blood i need, just as my soul writes the words for you to read. so if there is a chance that i do not find love, i'll always be able to look you in the eyes and tell you, maybe there is a possibility it finds me someday, when the sky is bare and the shine no longer invites me to stay. the mission in life is to live for a purpose and then die with a full heart. some of us get there and others

☾

wilt away because they never took time to fully understand how the seconds do not stop for us, even when life shits on us all. thus leaving words and feelings to slowly die in the dirt of which they are buried; hoping flowers of reason bloom with every season so that others can see and feel them when we are gone. they keep telling me, "if love doesn't exist, then what the hell are we living for anyway?" tomorrow, i will get dressed, eat breakfast, and go out looking for something i might not believe in, but dammit, i know it's out there somewhere between the shallow breaths i take and the wandering spaces my eyes get lost in. if you do not believe in it, believe in something worth breathing for.

this world needs your heartbeat.

☾

even if what we have should die,

i know when it is buried deep

beneath the crying skies, it will

give birth to something beautiful

that will live forever.

☾

she asked me, "do you think there's an expiration date in relationships?" i looked at her and said, "me personally, i believe we all have a date. whether it's the beginning or end to something. i don't call it an expiration date per se, but having been around my family and friends that have had parents divorce, i can tell you what they found to bring them together, before they eventually lost it along the way. i know things and events happen that can and will never be erased, which plays a paramount part, but in my opinion, love can be as easily lost as it is found. some move on with what is left and others try to sew and mend pieces that are forever left frayed by the past. they try and make sense of their new life so to speak, but remain in denial; making them lose their sense of reality. in a way we all have expiration dates, but i think we at times choose them ourselves; knowingly and unknowingly."

☾

she was born with this innate ability to
know when to rescue those who needed
saving. her hands reached down to the
pits that were dug below what humans
described as hell; a place where there is
no fire that burns you, only the memories
that you cannot escape and sirens who
sing the same song every night. it is
constant torture of maddening melodies,
but she pulled me out, and together we
rose like wildflowers in the desert. sometimes,
all it takes is someone who is willing to do the
impossible with you, for you to realize it's all in
your fucking head. do not fear what lives inside
of you. we all cage our demons differently.

☾

after a few months of being with her, she woke up one morning before i got up and went into the bathroom, but left the door open as if she wanted me to see something. ten minutes of looking in the mirror, she walked out with her hands full of tears, telling me, "i am not perfect." i asked her to come back to bed and i took her into my arms, and told her, "neither am i, and i do not need perfect, babe. i just need us."

☾

there's no reason for me to dream anymore. they now sleep next to me as the most beautiful thing these eyes have ever seen in this reality. she is there, and wherever i rest my soul, body, and mind, i know her euphoric heart will always be next to mine. i live for endless kisses, timeless passion, and an insatiable craving for only her.

while she held
my lifeless hand,
my last breath was
a dying whisper,

"love, was always in my words to you."

☾

right then was the only time i ever saw
the moon's reflection of another human.
she smiled at me from across the crowded
room, incessantly waving at me to make
sure i saw her. she was more than the love
of my life. she was everything the universe
told me she would be. with eyes made from
my wishes and a smile created by falling
stars, i constantly find myself trying to
discover and rediscover parts of her.
no matter where we are.

☾

there has never been anyone or anything
remotely close to giving me exactly what
you've put into my ever-growing heart.
without question, baby, you are not only
the best thing, but you are my entire sky
watching over me. i look up as often as i
can to see just how lovely you really are.
i am able to breathe and live in your
atmosphere; a place where i will always
fill my lungs with your sweet nothings.

☾

while the stars were talking
about us, they devised a
plan for you and i.

with the universe shifting and
folding itself, it lovingly pieced
together the corners of our
lives.

finally, after all of this time, i now
see and feel my purpose next to
me each and every night.

☾

it was not just falling in love for me. it was understanding i couldn't go to sleep without hearing her voice. it was knowing i needed her soul next to mine as i walked through life.
it was seeing the way she walked from the hallway into our bedroom wearing nothing at all, except a smile. i knew i loved her from the second i missed her when she told me, "goodnight."

her voice melted into me, and is now a part of my bloodstream.

☾

this cold house. this old mind
of mine. silence sneaks into the
cracks of where i once had my
walls built with concrete and
stone. an echo of a love song
plays on the outside, while i am
slow dancing with my own
shadow tonight.

the fireplace is lit and there are no
words to be said at this moment in
time.

for we shall wait until the moon gives
way to the sun, because i know in my
bones, it will love again.

(

if this is all there is
in life and all it can
give to me, then a
symphony of kisses,
being orchestrated
by our never-ending
laughter, will always
be my definition of
immortal happiness.

the way you say my name,

makes me want to find the

deepest spot inside of you,

and stay there.

☾

she asked me with wandering eyes,
"what do you see when you look at
me?" with the only answer i needed,
i softly told her, "i see hope in such a
way that i can finally experience it with
all six senses."

time, is the space between
where i am now and where
i have yet to travel. for some,
it's a journey carried out
alone, but with me, i know
you are here.

and you, my love, are timeless.

☾

we went to bed later than we usually do, but i wanted those few extra hours just to hold you. like a fragile flower needing comfort, my hands, heart, lips, and limbs found you, over and over again.

☾

we talk to each other as much
as life allows time to stand still.
it was in that moment where i
told her, "even when we are
not touching, we will always
be together."

that's what lovers do.
they continually hold
onto the heart, while
the rest of the world
searches for their
own.

☾

even the undulating clouds
taste like sweet and savory
vanilla when i am with her.

all the more reason for my
lips to never stop touching
her flesh.

it was how the trees blossomed with gorgeous red roses and the towering mountains cascaded the shadows of our unbreakable hearts that allowed me an opportunity to feel love in such a way that made me believe this place will always belong to the teachers and students of the word itself.

☾

then there was an explosion of energy between us that painted our souls with the colors of our love and marinated our hearts in the endless oceans of freedom that once flowed through our bones. we now roam wildly in a globe made by hope, where perspective is nothing more than living outside the lines that had once been drawn by those who said,

"reality is what happens when you open your eyes."

☾

the love for you that was born inside of me will never die. it burns with so much passion and desire, at times, consumes my very soul. just know wherever you are, i will always hold you with arms that were made for never letting go and a body that will always need you curled up beside it.

☾

there are days where i'm not sure if this
life of mine is even real. i awake to the
scent of her skin which is laced with the
fragrance of every ocean that makes up
who she is. i take my fingers and run them
up and down her spine, as i am constantly
learning how to play the keys which opens
her soul for a taste of the magic that
embodies it. when it is time to finally get
out of bed, we find that staying an extra five
minutes will always lead to ten, and then we
know another touch will be all that is needed
to experience the rough, but sensual desires
we crave; every morning before a single word
is said. we are us, and that is a rare fucking thing
to find these days.

just as you are
my first and last
thought, you
have and will
always be the
first true and
last heartbeat
within me.

☾

this much i hope you understand,
and that is the love i have for you
will always run through the winding
rivers of my blood. it is an endless
stream of passion and energy,
shocking my system with words that
jump from your tongue and land on
my skin. only you, darling, have ever
soaked into me. you are the hope my
eyes will always see and the reason
my life will never be empty. even when
they lower me down into the ground,
the earth will shake and tremble around
those who thought love was something
that could ever die.

☾

it's 8:40am and the fog is starting to roll in from the ocean. i think i will stay out here a little longer and wrap myself with it, begging it to engulf me the same way you do when we need each other. you are everywhere and even when i cannot see you, i feel you constantly throughout the day. it's one of my favorite things about us. even the universe knows a minute without you is too long of a wait, so it sends me the things you love as a reminder that you are always here with me.

☾

why do you think she isn't everything
you are? is it because she has outlasted
every doubt that has ever crept into your
mind, or is it basically the fact that she's
too fucking real for your childish soul?
maybe those who cannot see the pure
perfection in humans that seem different,
should learn to understand the image you
see in the mirror, is only a reflection of your
own imagination.

(

as i tied her
hands behind
her back with
my words,
i got on my
knees and
began to
undress her
soul with my
lips. it was a
coming
together of two
wild and fiery
humans
needing fierce
and powerful
love.

(

i love mornings with you, my love.

your voice sends me over the edge

and it's such a beautiful fall as i land

closer to you each time.

☾

i know the journey i seek, lies within

you and me. places we have yet to

see together will one day become a

traveling guide for the dreams we

share.

☾

every chance i get, i will always love to lay with you naked;

body to body. bones to bones. soul to soul.

in the purest of all forms, we are the moments others talk about. the ones where heartbeats actually do transcend reality.

☾

i will love you until the stars fade
from our sight and the earth melts
away. i will love you through each
storm we chase and each calming
breeze that hits our face.
through the waves and over the
mountains, i will continue to put
one foot and one hand in front of
the other, allowing us both to know
we were created to have matching
shadows. we are more than just two
humans who are in love. we are souls
cast down by the heavens for others
to learn from. we are more than just
two sets of hands and two sets feet
with the same heartbeat. we are the
everlasting picture of what it means
when words cannot describe how it
feels to be on fire, but more than alive
at the same time.

☾

last night, we stood
before each other,
naked as stars and
totally vulnerable
as the imperfect
humans we are.

going to sleep that night,
we took off our skin and
slept in our bones without
ever losing eye contact.

you and i are connected like that.

☾

what you have given to me over the time we have been talking, is more than anyone has ever given before. i believe we are all created with a purpose and a hidden love we all search for throughout our existence. maybe one day i can form the sentences that can show you this to be true. until then, the trust you have allowed me to hold, is everything i could hope for. we trust each other, not only with words, but conversations unheard of by those who are closest to us; secrets shared that have never breathed the same air as we are inhaling now. trusting is more than just understanding each other. it is allowing the soul to feel loved and appreciated.

☾

i often wonder how i have
lived this life without ever
knowing of you before.
but now that i do, i will
never be able to breathe
the same again.

through the heart and out
the soul is now the pattern
of never letting go.

☾

maybe forever is only a shared breath that allows your heart to finally beat with a purpose. maybe it is a person who is there for you when the entire universe seems to be against you and they stay because they believe in fighting for someone who has always fought for them. maybe forever is a lasting impression of a soulful journey through the madness raging in and out of control around us all. forever is whatever you choose it to be. for me, forever is you, and i will always know where to find it when today isn't long enough to tell you just how much you mean to me. though my knuckles might get bloodied, i will stand in front of you, until we are both safe and there is no such thing as being alone. you will never be by yourself in this world, darling. i am always there for you and with you. you and i are fighters and that will never change.

☾

i will love you gently, with both hands and all of me. i will love you as i am now with you; entirely perfect in such a peaceful way. taking my time to admire such a lovely human, i will love you and spoil you because that's what i know and that's what i need to do. so just relax, lay back, and let me take you in, while my lips create paragraphs full of hope and sin. i cannot promise you all of the finer things most of the world consumes on a daily basis. all i can do is love you with what i have and that is a soul which was created to show you how you are to be treated all of the time. just like the distinguished butterfly landing on the petal of a red rose, it holds it, and the universe captures a moment of life invisible to those who do not love with each of their senses. they miss out on the perfection, because they do not see everything the way it is supposed to be seen. sometimes, you have to put your heart to the ground to value the meaning of existence and feel it.

☾

you taught me how to finally be happy with
myself and i hope that i have done the same
for you. in the end, it is exactly what you
have always deserved; in heart, mind, and spirit.
you are a wild soul without boundaries and a
world that is unexplored. always live your life like
that, sweetheart. it is endearing.

☾

she often wondered what it was
i saw in her that made me love
her so much. today she asked
me and i told her,

"i see your heart, babe."

sometimes, it's the things we
cannot see ourselves that
truly mean the most to
others.

hearts are crazy things.
sometimes they beat
for everything and
other times they beat
for absolutely nothing
at all but a second
chance.

☾

if i should ever forget something, just know i am still learning how to remember.

it has been so long since i've had someone to care for and adore in such a way.

i forgot what it meant and how it feels to carry a heart that was not my own.

i am trying, and that's one thing i will always do for you, for us.

☾

this morning felt like a day of which all things made sense to me. for the first time in over ten years, i woke up without needing a cigarette. so if you see me in the streets, walking and breathing, i am finally taking a breath and a chance that finally has meaning.

no filters.
no smoke.
no matches.

just a soul full of everlasting hope and countless dreams to get me where i need to be.

now, i am free.

☾

two kinds of
humans roam
this universe:

those who judge and those who
understand. i loved her because
she cared enough to wrap her
arms around me and tell me it
is okay to trust again.

☾

i fell to the floor with you. only this time,
i chose to stay on the ground beside you.
there i could finally see what you needed.
you desired someone to remain by your side
through the restless times, even when it hurt
to hold you. i am unfamiliar with that type of
worried pain, but i am always willing to give
you my everything. i gathered you in my loving
arms to help ease the trouble surrounding your
anxious heart. we were together on the cold and
unforgiving floor, talking about nothing at all.
except to us, it was not the words as much as it
was the pure comfort of having each other to
hold. we talked, we kissed, and we made love
feel like an outsider, looking in through the
prism of life; wondering how we got there.
a sensation we both will forever covet.

if you are in pain, i am in pain.

☾

as soon as we opened the door,
my taste for her was overwhelming,
and she knew it. she pulled me in
close and whispered in my ear two
words i needed to hear, "take me."
so i picked her up and she wrapped
her legs around my waist tightly so
she could hold on. we began walking
up the walls, because we knew we could
not make the stairs. i knew they might not
be able to hold us up, but our fire for each
other was going to burn down the house
either way.

☾

after a long evening and even after me sleeping through our first fight, i woke up early to make her breakfast. she loved orange juice and hash browns, so i brought them to her. as she rolled over to see me, i told her that she will always have my heart and how bad i felt for making her upset. i then said something i've never told anyone before,

"i am not just here for you. i am alive for you, sweetheart."

all hearts bleed the same.

it is the reason why they beat

that makes them different.

☾

i'm not sure if i wanted a life
without pain or a life full of
love, but i knew the heart
and soul that were encased
by her flesh and bones
would always provide me with
both. she was my saving grace
and my hallelujah, wrapped in
gypsy magic.

☾

i have yet to experience a single day with you and i am already completely terrified of losing you. all it will take is a single touch from you and our bodies will align with our souls, thus creating a symmetrical sensation needed for a balanced life full of random moments and indescribable passion every time we are near each other. being afraid of losing something you never had, now that's a powerful statement. one of which will make having that person mean so much more to you and doing everything you can for them. not because they asked you to, but for the simple reason of finally understanding the moments spent with them will always make life worth fighting for.

good morning, love.

in my life, i have never had a moment that i couldn't articulate in some way. all of that changed last night. i hope when it is my time to leave this universe, i am allowed to take the echo of your voice with me. i guess when a moment is too perfect to describe, the heart keeps most of it to itself, providing the body with a feeling of which needs not to be shared with anyone else. you and i experienced a shifting of souls, and to me, nothing else needs to be said. this is ours, and for the first time, i believe trying to illustrate this with anymore detail would do it an injustice.

everything life had

ever taken away from

me, she gave it all back

and then some when she

took a chance and stayed.

☾

i reached down through
the gateway of my throat,
with both of my committed
hands to haul up the words
i needed to tell you.

one hand clutched my soul
and the other grabbed my
heart.

"please do not return them
to me. they belong to you."

☾

there are nights where i swear
i feel you breathing on me and
telling me, "i need you."
though you are not here right
now, your voice is a reminder
i have someone who cares for
me. whether i am alone in my
thoughts, busy working on
another piece of writing, or just
making breakfast, i miss you.

we have to learn how to build
cities in our hearts with highways
leading to our minds and travel
there every fucking chance we get.
in order to become all of the dreams
i wish, that is where i shall live and
grow; amongst the population of
hope that inhabits the open road.

☾

the car drives itself nowadays. there's no direction i can go without feeling rejected and blind. this world has got a hold of me and will not allow my hands to steer the wheel into the sea. i just want to go back to where i came from.

a place where i know i belong.

☾

the difference between me and every other guy you might meet, is that i will still love you when your eighty. i will still hold your hand, because i love the way it feels when our love is shown to the world. i will still kiss you goodnight and hold you close to me, because that's where you have always belonged. i will still open every door we go through, allowing you to enter first, because i want the room to see what beautiful is supposed to look like. and when we both have to say goodbye, we will know that the life we had shared together, was only the beginning to our dance. i will see you soon, my love.
i promise.

☾

she was created from the ashes of the phoenix
and born to do the impossible. her relentless
courage and will, took her places no other
human could go. she was never alone,
because love lived in her heart, and
home was always a place in her soul.

(

i will love you naked or clothed in the
beauty you so elegantly wear. i will love
all of your parts that can be seen with my
tender eyes and felt by my benevolent heart.
i will love you as the days turn into years
and as each season changes the colors of
my life.

you are all that i know and all i wish to
understand in this universe. i love you
for all of the ways you allow me to feel
and hold your soul. i love you, because
you've built a new world inside of me
we can call our own.

☾

this is not a poem. this is a reflection note. parts of my past are littered with darkness and decisions that have shaped me and molded my soul into what and who you see today. i am not proud of them and i do not write this to act as if i am, but i am thankful to still be able to breathe in this air around me. before you, i was ashamed of it all. only a handful of people actually know everything that has happened to me. i keep pieces of my life to myself and to those who make up my circle; it is a very small circle. then something happened. before i had said a single word, i trusted you. this overwhelming sensation came over me and i felt peace and the calm i had been searching for. when we started talking, i put it all out there for you, thinking you would run, because how could one stay after hearing everything i told you. i had no reason

☾

to hide my cards. i needed you to be able to see what i was looking at. you listened to me and never once have you judged me. i've had so many fucking sleepless nights, worrying about and thinking about what things i have done wrong and spending such little time focusing in on all i have done right. you have come into my life and allowed me a chance to rid my past and burn down the closet that once housed all of my skeletons. the ashes have been spread across the very ground i have walked away from. hoping one day those who have dealt with the same obstacles and trials in their lives can look down and see where new beginnings come from. moving on and accepting what was and learning how to get to where you need to go is one of the most crucial aspects in life. i wish for the day that we all get there, and if you're already there, i hope you can help others who need it.

☾

i will never be apprehensive when it
comes to showing the love i have for
you in any public place. i'll hold your
hand and touch your face while i get
lost in our kiss. i'll grab you and pull
you in close to me so others can
witness love on display in an open
space. maybe one day the world will
learn that being with someone you
cannot live without, means never letting
go of them, no matter who's in the crowd.

☾

with you, i will
never wander
this world alone
or lost.

i'll always be
exactly where
i was made to
breathe, live,
and love.

☾

a broken home.

it raised me and set a new foundation underneath my feet that gave a child at the time, years of perspective in order to appreciate not always having the best situation. it was a teacher to me and no matter how much i despised it and wanted to tear it down, it taught me day in and day out, how to care and give to others, because giving is the ultimate gift of being a human. knowing i might not get everything back i have given over the years, my heart will remain full of precious love and unwavering understanding that sometimes life will present itself in the cruelest of forms to let you know you are strong enough to build wherever you wish to grow. even if you are

☾

not old enough to comprehend the plans,
the sketches you need are in the people
you meet. they are walking structures built
from pain, love, heartache, and happiness,
living amongst the tallest of trees and buildings
in this world. do not continue to tear down the
brokenness around you. build with what and
who is around you. we are all given a specific
set of tools to create with. use them and use
them often. you never know what kind of
monuments can be restored and given new
life to help others see the beauty surrounding
the cracks in us all.

☾

i crave the deepest parts of you.

the places where i can go to stretch

my soul out and relax with the soothing

sounds of your butterflies harmonizing

with mine.

☾

she taught me that even the most broken of souls can find peace from the pieces left behind after the war within oneself. she not only helped me gather them, but she molded them together with such savoring love that i knew i would never have to battle alone ever again. i now wear it as a shield that i carry with me every day to let those know who have been defeated once or twice before. losing a battle does not define you. what defines you is, going back in for more, knowing this time the outcome will be different because you finally believe in yourself. it's that action that separates the weak and strong minded.

(

i cried last night.

not because of sadness or agony, but for the simple reason and pure joy of knowing i have never truly been this happy. it's hard to put into words really, but all i can tell you is, these eyes have never looked at something so clear and saw a reflection they loved more than the one they now see. she has allowed the season of my spirit to change from winter to summer in a matter of months.

and it is finally warm again.

☾

i found you amongst the scattered chaos in my life. you helped me understand just what a beautiful mess it actually was.

both of our hands touched hearts that night, and with that, we will never know what it is like to feel anything ever again.

for once you have touched love, nothing will ever feel the same.

(

the key to life is having a steady balance,
while maintaining a structure around you
that is acceptable to adapt. this entire life
of mine, i have been walking tightrope after
tightrope, trying to make sure that if i did fall,
i would learn a lesson of how to enhance my
mind, my breathing, and the total perspective
of everything and everyone around me. i have
to a certain degree, but when i met you i knew
everything would change. the way i lived my life,
to the way my heartbeat sounds when it hears
your voice, to the way i stand as tall and alive

☾

as any redwood in a forest full of falling leaves.
down to the very reason of why my eyes open
in the morning, and that is knowing you are
here helping me. you provided me with the
balance needed so i could get back on life's
track and remain entirely free from the
negativity that had once surrounded me.
it was you, who once and for all suffocated
my demons with love, and now i am a free
man again; prospering with a balance that
had once kept me uneven.

in my eyes, she can do no wrong.
this close-minded of a place is not
big enough to hear her song.

she is not afraid to say what she
means and if you choose to blink,
you will miss her reaching out to
take all that she needs.

☾

maybe not today, tomorrow, next month,
or even three years from now, but one day
i will learn your taste, your smell, and your
touch. i will devour every inch of your soul
in order to understand and put away into
my mind forever, all of the places you have
longed to feel alive, kissed, and held. for when
the time comes and i can no longer breathe you
in and hold you deep within my lungs, i know i
will have not only experienced love, but you and
i grew it in all of the places that had once been
burned by others. i will continually do this until
the only thing left of me is your memory,
guiding me back to you.

that's a goddamn promise.

☾

when i was 11 years old, i promised
myself that i would find something
i believed in with with my entire being
and love more than i could ever imagine.

i was not sure if i could be able to do that
after growing up the way i did, but now i am
at a point in my life where i can finally see just
how damn lucky i have been to have found not
just one thing, but two things i wholeheartedly
believe in and love more than i have ever
known.

life will take you places, sometimes the worst
ones imaginable in order for you to experience
and appreciate the lessons of never giving up
and staying true to who you are. even when i
was at my worst, i knew the best of me would
always shine through, because i believed in me,
before anyone else ever did.

☾

she was not looking for acceptance from anyone, because her life was built on her rules; a place where birds danced with the wind and the oceans sang of her songs.

it is where love grows from the flowers she has planted and now waters daily with sweet lullabies. the sun shines brighter and the moon stays out longer, just so she can have the time to relish both sides of the world.

do you ever get that feeling where you know everything is falling into place? well i have, and it has been going on for five days now. it feels like anxiety, but it is not the kind that makes me worry. i have yet to experience this before and i am trying to understand it and make sense of it. considering my life has always been about change and adapting to those around me and to the places i have lived, this feeling is a sense of comfort and the kind

☾

of peace that kills off my demons and allows for the angels to dance on my shoulder. i know one reason why i feel this way, you. you have let me become so much more than just another someone. you have given my heart a fullness it has never encountered before. one that can overflow and i know nothing will be wasted. i am not sure what the other part to the equation is and why this feeling has taken over me. i am still figuring it out, but its a damn good place to be; somewhere i never saw myself until i met the

☾

woman in my dreams. i've thought about the places we could travel and i know california is a destination we would both like to end up at. i'll write your name in the sand and you can watch the water go around it, because i am protecting not only you, but everything that is us. we can finally dance in the ocean like we have talked about and get lost in the sun as it shines through our souls and projects the hearts of lovers. i have a feeling i'll be seeing you sooner than we both know. my intuition is hardly ever wrong. i guess i figured out the other part to that equation after all;

☾

the kind where two always equals love.
and when you feel like you have lost
everything and you cannot move your
feet to get where you need to be, i will
be there, helping you along the way.
and when the darkest of night skies
surround you and there are no stars
to speak to, i'll bring them out for you,
proving once and for all that together,
they live inside of us. there is nothing in
this

☾

world we can't do and with the love we have molded from our past lives, it is the strongest and most resilient kind there is. we will not lose, because our love will outlast death and continue to grow on the branches of hope. nothing ever truly dies. it just finds a new way to be born again.

☾

it is a quarter after three and you are still here with me. you talk as if you have never been tired in your life. i am oblivious to the fact that we are now exactly where i imagined us in my dreams; in my bed, having the talk that will catapult us into our new beginning. it is not a dream others would have, but to me, the best part is, i never have to close my eyes again in order to see you. for i am living out my dream as we stay awake until nine-thirty in the morning. oh, how i wish clocks were hand-less and time knew when to just leave us the hell alone.

the moon will
always remind
me of you.
wherever you go,
i know that it will
forever have your
glow.

☾

if you ever find a message in
a bottle from me, this is what
it would read:

i was never lost at sea, just a little lost in my mind. to whom ever is reading this, i hope you are fine. life is too short to worry about today. i threw this into the sea to ease my heart. when your are done, put the message back in and return this bottle to the sea, so it can help someone again, just as it did with me.

☾

the gifts you've given to me,
have your fingerprints all over
them. if there are days where
we cannot touch, my hands
will never forget how it feels
to hold yours with the precise
care and love needed to show
you how much you mean to
me.

☾

i feel eyes follow me everywhere i go. i hear their thoughts as if they were speaking out loud on this busy street. for i was cursed with a mind that has tentacles that reach out to the lonely, only to be touched by them myself, as soon as i try and take a breath to keep up with the pace at which they are being felt.

☾

i often wonder while sitting at a restaurant, who actually waits on them. when they leave their jobs at night, do they have someone that leaves a tip for them, or do they go home to an empty house where shattered dreams hang in a closet, next to the shoe-box full of broken hearts?

☾

sitting here, listening to these old men tell their fishing stories is something i thoroughly enjoy. to love something so much is a blessing few ever grasp before it is too late. most humans do not get the chance to see their 60's or 70's. as my ears pay close attention, i hear knowledge of which i learned when i was a kid. remembering back to when my grandfather would tell those same "big fish" stories. i sure do miss him. for he was a story teller unlike myself. i always seemed to forget the punch line every time, but he made words come to life. making you believe that he once caught a mermaid. "i only used my looks and she couldn't resist getting into my boat." he would always end that tale by saying, "never forget your hook, line, or sinker. you never know which one you will have to use."

☾

i want all of your mistakes. for i will not try and cover them up like other guys who left you. i need to see all of your scars, so that i can show you all of mine for you to know we have shared the same pain. what this universe has done to you, it has done to me, over and over again. i never wanted a perfect life. i just wanted your imperfections to know and understand mine.

my butterflies still circle my insides with such
vigor and determination to never rest until
they can be kept alive inside your own heart.
it is their home and i am temporarily a keeper
to the one thing in life that will always keep me
up. knowing you are not here to share the wind
they generate, allows me to fly for you.

☾

hidden between the valleys of her heart, lives a beautiful red rose that grows beside a cherry tree. it blooms every day, even without the water that is needed. it waits for the sun every morning, just to feel its radiant light of love.

as night approaches, it closes itself to the universe, allowing only the one who cares for it, to see it in a vulnerable state.

carve my heart
with your name.
i want to hear it
with each beat
that's played.
a gentle lullaby
for me, so when
i sleep, i will
always hear you
next to me.

☾

i regret not kissing you goodnight,

the night before i left. if i had never

felt a sorrowful moment up until

that point, i was greeted by one

when i woke up without you.

life was meant for us to be weird and to break the mold that us humans were meant to forever live ordinary lives. if we succumb to this ideology, we will completely destroy ourselves. when in fact, we should be building a life worth of infinite meaning and wisdom for others to learn from. never set out to be another normal face in the crowd. do what you have to in order to stand out and make a name for yourself, instead of taking someone else's life and applying it to your own.

be independent from dependency.

☾

you will forever be a bookmark in my life.
where i go back to see when times were
right and the nights could never last
long enough. we had the world dancing
to the sound of our love and watching it
through the kaleidoscope made from stars.
it was our masterpiece, which was painted
by the times of our lives; using memories to
color in the outlines of the pictures in our
hearts.

☾

my scars have been stepping stones for me. they have provided a story for others to read. for i am not proud of them all, but some of them were worth the endless fall back to reality. as i continue to collect them through these trying times, i know in the end, life should never be able to break you.

no matter how far you fall.

☾

i was once told at an early age, "you will never be able to wake a soul that was made to live dormant." i never agreed with this statement and never gave it any life. just because it has not been done yet doesn't mean you should not try. everyone deserves an opportunity to experience at least a second of falling in love with everything beautiful this world has to offer. we all deserve to have our hearts experience the flame that reaches down from the sky and creates the fire in our souls.

☾

we once stretched our souls
out to reach each side of the
two lonely oak trees in order
to release the stress our
bodies were under.

we were swaying back and
forth from the whispering
wind that came along and
gave us the fresh air we
needed to feel alive
once again.

(

at night, when we are done making love,
she goes over to the corner and plays the
piano in the dark. with every ivory key she
strikes, my heart begins to sync; creating
the baseline for another after-dark session
of making up for lost time.

we celebrate now, even after all of the years
we constantly said goodbye to one another.
but we always knew how to find each other
again, regardless of the places we were in.

all it took was the absence of touch, to actually
feel again.

☾

the ink you see transformed into words on this paper, are for the eyes of many. but the ones we speak quietly together, while sharing and basking in our moments, will never touch this surface. for those are the ones i will only whisper in your ear, sweet one.

☾

these damn
crows have
continued to
walk all over
me with their
unforgiving
feet.
leaving their
mark for the
world to see
just how
tiresome being
alone can be.

do not fear being alone in this life.

for it is during those priceless moments,

we finally stop looking for someone or

something, and start to focus on who we

need to be to make life worth the breaths

we take.

☾

do you know why i love you?

it's because you have always made me
feel as if i am finally worthy of someone's
unconditional love and never want to let
go of me. i say this to you now while
standing in a room full of broken humans,
listening to their screams penetrate my
heart. one day we will all feel what it is like
to have someone who is able to hug the
insecurities that we carry around our soul.
i used to beg and plead to the universe,
wishing i could experience what being
complete felt like. now i have you for the
rest of my life. together we will become our
own paradise of everyday memories;
being brilliant suns in a world full of
darkened days.

(

i've always had friends tell me throughout
my life, "never give your heart to anyone.
they always end up dropping it."

i always laughed it off, thinking to myself,
"maybe it is true, but on the other hand,
we often drop our own hearts."

☾

we all harbor a soul that is longing to catch
fire and ignite those who are lost and broken.

do not allow other humans to smother
and put out what the universe created.

we are all of one body, mind, and spirit
chosen to walk a life full of adventure.

do not regret a memory made, but savor
the taste of which it gave you. long for
that every time you open your eyes and
go drink from the well that holds the
dripping magic from the stars.

to go through life knowing i'll never be able
to touch you in the places still buried deep
beneath your soul, will always be a tragedy
i never knew could exist with someone
who they have yet to hold.

but i guess that's what dreams are for.

☾

i have found a new muse. one that finally took the place of you. though she is just a shadow for now, she walks through life unafraid of the holes in my soul and fills them with her fingers.
not everyone needs saving. they just need a love that will follow them, even if the sun cannot find them. she is my white whale, who is caught in the net of my dreams. i know that i will never be able to fully bring her to life, but the distance we share in-between breaths is enough for me to hope she can hear me breathing for her.

☾

i love how she would leave
feathers in our bed when
it was time for her to go.

allowing me a chance to hold
a tiny piece of her next to me,
whilst trying to go back to
sleep without the angel
from my dreams.

for tonight, we shall dance

with our demons and ask

them what haunts them

for once.

sometimes it is

easier being alone,

rather than thinking

you're happy.

☾

it was our scars that brought you and i together.
they needed us to love each other for them to
finally heal. never again shall we be afraid of
what other people might say or think about
our life. our story does not involve them nor
will it ever make sense to those who fail to
understand that scars will always be life
written on flesh.

they are simply words not everyone can read.

☾

the dilemma was always me trying to love myself more than the next day. if i did not, how could i ever love you more and give you everything you needed when the reflection i saw in the mirror was telling me that i would never be enough for anyone.

bi-polar and depression get the best of me at times and i have to realize those are just words and not who i have to be. though to love you with all of me, you will have to accept my faces you see in the mirror. those damn things seem to always change color; no matter if the light is on or off.

hold my hand, sweetheart, and allow me to feel your strength. it gets lonely when your shadow is the only one dancing amongst a crowded, jubilant street.

every now
and then
you have
to air your
soul out
and allow
it to taste
the breeze
of life.

(

i know i do not have the perfect smile.
i understand i have never had the
perfect past that others claim
they do.

i am a sinner and i am not ashamed of
the things i've done. i am here now
and i am perfect for the ones who
never left, and because of that,
my definition of perfect will
never be like yours.

judge me and smother me in your
callous words, but i will always
have a life worth meaning,
even if you cannot read
the writings

☾

i've painted throughout the walls of my
life. i love who i am and where i am
going is unknown right now yet i
am still walking, breathing, and
burning down the road behind
me so others who left, will
never find me.

i am not perfect, hell, nothing about me
is and that's the way i like it. an imperfect
soul is an incredible human once you get
to know them. for i am still working on
how not to be perfect, because that is
being normal. why would anyone
want to be that?

☾

i never thought my love for you
could outdo the moon's love for
the sea. sometimes i wish you
could completely wash over
me and drown me with a
love creating our own
gravity;

where we could drink the same
feelings and breathe the same
air.

all i ask is if you are to love me,
please drown me with your
soul.

☾

the great thing about life is, there is only one of you ever created. so why do we constantly try and emulate others and pretend we are someone we were not meant to be. the fact that there is no one else in this universe like you, should make you feel pretty damn special. being yourself might not be fun at times, but it will always be worth it to enjoy a life meant for you.

go and live without looking back.
nothing will ever be worth your
time when you are constantly
rewinding old memories.

☾

all hearts are created equal,
but some tend to give more
and share parts of it filled
with endless amounts of love
and sacrifice.

never be ashamed of your
heart. for it already knows
too much and will never
ask for anything in
return.

☾

whether or not it is possible or even practical,

life should always be about creating smiles and

feelings; bringing them to life for others that

need them at this very moment in time.

☾

as individuals, we humans are
just pieces of a universal puzzle.
we are scattered all throughout
this world, trying to become a
meaning and find a definition
that suits our lives.

if only we could come together
and stand as one, who knows
what we could do. who knows
what we could become.

☾

maybe all we will ever be are a few lines in life's book of adventures, but darling, it would be the best damn short story anyone would ever read. at times, all it takes is a moment of love to transcend a lifetime of pain. for when our page is finally read by those who never believed in their own story, they will be satisfied with our lines. not everything will be a novel in life.

some of the most breathtaking and beautiful moments happen within those few seconds of breathing in and breathing out.

just find your

happiness and

never look back.

life is too short

and precious of

a thing to do

anything else,

but love it.

☾

she has always been the collection
of my wishes, who wears the stars
that made me fall for her.

she's my constellation of love and
i will continue to wish for her every
day, until we both become a part
of the sky;

a sacred place where the sun and moon
touch, hoping for another chance to see
one another again.

she was not the type of woman that needed
attention. all she ever yearned for in life
was an opportunity to create her own destiny.
it never mattered what kind of soil she was
planted in or how much water she could obtain,
in her mind, a chance was all it would take to
withstand the pain of being excluded from a
world where the color of your petals define you.
all it takes in life is an open mind and full heart
to see past the differences you think set us all
apart. look closely and observe the environment
surrounding you. it might turn out to be right
where you have always meant to exist.

☾

there are words and ideas i wish to not only tell you, but show you as well. i want you to be able to feel them as much as they have continued to embrace me over the years. if you stay, then i will never leave you or your feelings behind. where we are going, only the stars truly know, but i am confident when i tell you that love has saved me and kept me alive long enough to tell you this tonight. i love you, and no matter what happens in the seconds and minutes after this, my lips want to dance with yours, and kiss what has always been my drug. you are not only my life, you completely own my heart and all that is left inside. i love you, because deep down those are the words and feelings that have embraced me all throughout my entire life.

☾

when her beautiful heart broke, the angels cried and mourned for someone they had watched over and protected since she was born. that night, they gave her heart the wings it needed to fly again. knowing this time they would protect it from the inside, she would be able to soar above the pain of yesterday. with each successful flight, she has something to hold onto at night. she now has the determined strength to live again, while the angels continue to guard a sacred heart.

one of which they will never allow to break again.

☾

even after the greatest tragedy you experience in life, a seed of understanding is planted in the soil of your soul; allowing hope to take root and grow wildly throughout your dreams. do not stay in the section of your mind that breeds sadness or depression. believe it will get better and never forget to water the seed. even the smallest of life needs water to penetrate the concrete flesh around it.

☾

when my heart skips and is out of

rhythm, i want to believe it is

because of the breath you

forgot to take.

☾

even if i never meet you.

even if we never touch hands.

even if our lips never share a single

secret between our souls, i know that

i am better because of you.

☾

you know, i've probably loved a lot of the wrong people in my life and truly cared for everyone that either despised me or never wanted to understand me. and to me, that is life. continuing to love and care for someone in which they will never fully understand the reasons behind it all, makes me want to try even harder. i will fall, and i know the world will be there to catch me when it happens, but it will not deter me from trying my damnedest to make this universe a better place for the future generations to come who are still being taught what love and sincerity means. most of the time, the honest truth is viewed as taboo, yet to me, it is the only way to learn. make mistakes, continue to love those you can, and never give up on anyone, because i know how hard it is when a soul gives up on a human.

in order to
build character,
even the
strongest of
things must
become weak
at some point.

☾

i once knew a man who would sit at a random street corner every day, handing out pennies. what others did not know was that this man used to be a millionaire and one of the wealthiest humans in the city.

"i heard a voice one night in which it told me to make a difference in this world. so i started giving away my fortune to those less fortunate than me."

his last pennies were not a sign of his bank account. they were a sign of trust and hope for others that needed it. even a penny can make someone rich. adding pennies to your life will eventually lead you to the dollars you need in order to believe anything is possible if you take time to appreciate even the simplest form of kindness.

☾

my heart seems to be an orphan these
days. where all it looks for is people to
love and care for it, instead of handing
it off and passing it to someone else
who doesn't want it either. but i will
become better, because of those who
continue to leave me at random times in
my life, searching for something they think
is better. when you do, let me know how
that works out for you; having a shell of a
heart that pretends to be willing to fill it
with unspoken words and neglected
feelings.

mine will always be overflowing with the vibes,
love, and words unknown to most. if you
cannot hold my truth in your heart,
do not ask me to give mine to
you in return.

☾

i'll never be able to
give you the life you
want, but together,
we can both give
each other the time
we need to decide
what it is we're
really after.

our love had stars knocking
on our hearts, asking us what
makes it so beautiful and how
we keep our shine so bright.
for others cannot see what love
actually does on the inside of you
and i, making what we have more
than special.

we are not strangers.

we are simply humans

with the same vibe that

have yet to meet in this

life.

☾

all i wanted to do was love you,
and if that's all i could wish for
in this life then i hope there is
enough magic floating around
us to land on our hearts and
make it happen.

(

maybe that's the point,
to leave as many broken
pieces as you can behind
for others to find so they
know it is okay when life
breaks you. our fragments
create whole reasons for
those who seek
understanding.

☾

the only time i've ever felt
suffering, is when she almost
decided to leave my life.

my heart dropped to the bottom
of my soul and my knees fell to
the ground as if i had never
known how to walk before.

thinking that you might lose your
ability to love again, is one of the
most intense feelings that exists.

☾

drugs, alcohol, and self-inflicted wounds take so many of us too soon.

do not be afraid to say what is on your mind.

no one is more important than the next yet we live our lives as if it's true.

we are enough. remember that.

(

my parents taught me what love is not.
now i live with the words and images
of those days and nights.

love is understanding and will always be
there even if the sheets cover your face.

they are the greatest shield for a kid
who sees more when their door
is closed to the reality actually
taking place outside

☾

we were goddamn magic together and for
those who couldn't see it, who couldn't see
how beautiful it was, they were the ones
looking up at the night sky in complete
disbelief asking themselves, "how can it be?
how can love be brushed by the hands of the
universe without making any mistakes?"
the reason is, everything you think you can
see, already exists in the minds of those who
believe in unforeseen energy;

the push and pull existence you and i make
love in every night.

☾

there are times where i shouldn't say
half the things i tell you, but i have never
been good at hiding emotions. i'm sure
there is a reason for that, but for now it is
something i am learning to project in a way
that makes sense and not just more particles
for your brain to depict as something everyone
says eventually. i want my words to be different.
i need them to be. if not, i will be like everyone
else you have ever met.

☾

whatever she was doing,

it allowed my heart to finally

rest. she had this finite way of

settling my nerves while creating

fire underneath my skin.

☾

when i was growing up, i was neither
rich or poor, just a middle class kid.
i have an older and a younger brother,
so being the middle child was always
interesting and i had my own way of
surviving the chaos. it feels like i am
floating between the earth and the stars,
wandering off to talk to the moon again
to see if she knows how it feels to be in
different places of the world at once.

we as the human race have created ways to explore the very depths of the darkness that the universe calls home. we've invented sophisticated tools to reach into the deepest parts of the ocean and the highest peaks of the mountains in the world. but here we are as society, still making the same damn mistakes, day after bloody day. there is beautiful art walking the streets of humanity, completely lost, because they have not even been asked a question about their lives. so really, are we doing everything we can to learn about what makes us the individuals we are? explore a soul every once and a while. you might find out that they need help, or hell, maybe they need a favor. whatever the case may be, search to find communication through spoken word, instead

☾

of reading it on a screen. we as humans need to understand where we are going all depends on those to the left and right of us. we are all waiting to be discovered by someone and today is the perfect day just for that. traveling as much as i did when i was younger, gave me the opportunity to take in a variety of different cultures and countless encounters with an abundant amount of amazing humans. everywhere i've been, lives in my bones and will forever be a part of who i am. to me, that's the greatest gift there is; growing and learning that in a chaotic yet beautiful way, we all come from

(

the same place. once we comprehend such a complex idea, the better off the world will be once we start building structures above our heads, instead of burying each other with words and actions that will be written in some form or fashion on a stone trying to explain what was left behind for others to visit and read.

if you ever find yourself visiting mine, leave a bottle of whiskey and two cups so we can have a drink and discuss what you are doing to make a change, instead of missing me.

☾

my life has been comprised of dark nights and darker days at times. though right now at this very moment, the sun has never seemed so bright. the past few months have been a life changing experience for me and i never thought i would see the day where my heart would beat for someone else again. but i can honestly say i feel needed for the first time in over six years. it is a feeling i hope we all get to experience in our lives. it needs to be felt; the feeling of meaning. the absolute definition of being alive. i am not sure how long it will last, just as i am not sure if tomorrow will greet us when we wake up. though for now,
this second, happiness fills my soul.

☾

she was the flower who was afraid

of blooming and opening up for

the world to see the intricate ways

she was made. created for the sun

and worshiped by many, i loved her

for all that she was and everything

she believed she needed to be.

she was created to walk through fields
of the most elegant colors of the world.
with her wandering feet, she painted
a drifting landscape where others
could follow if they wanted to in order
to witness and start believing in change.

the painting is an ongoing masterpiece,
but with time, we all can walk together
creating hope in an abandoned
wilderness of imagination.

☾

at the beach today, the tide was out, allowing the birds to dig in the soggy bottom of the earth. i noticed a few birds digging with their beaks and scrapping at the dirt, trying to uncover any type of food
to eat.
i passed them three or four times while i was riding. as i made my way back to the house, i wondered, "when was the last time i got my hands dirty or worked tirelessly for something i desperately needed."
i then looked at my hands and decided it had been too damn long since the last time they fought for something or tried to discover a reason to bleed with the stars.

(

she gave
me
something
nobody
else
could ever
give me;
a future

☾

you told me how
much you loved
the rain,

so i showered you
with words from
my soul until
you needed
to hold
me.

together as one, we danced
on a page and made love on
an idea formed from our
hearts.

☾

i look forward to the day where two glasses, two plates, and two hearts are at the table, talking about life. a conversation between lovers is unlike anything else.

everything is passionate.
everything leads to a
random moment where
a single kiss is captured
by the universe when
nothing else can be
said.

☾

in life,
it's when
all else fails
that we learn
how to hold
on completely.

☾

as i say this
to you now,
all i want to
do is hold
you with
everything i
have left to
give.
maybe then
i won't fall
apart like
everyone
else.

(

i often wonder to myself, not so much out loud, but i try and switch things up, because at times it is way too fucking insane in there for me to even conjure up an idea, more less a relevant response to the question. amongst the spiraling winds calling out to me and the ravishing waves breaking the surf, i ask, "what in the hell was i created for?" was it to be alone and think these thoughts or was it to run underneath the sun, moon, and stars, never surrendering until i find my calling? maybe i should write more and think less, but either way these words will always find a place in the sand, waiting for the love of the ocean to soothe my ache from this world. i also find myself thinking of ways to better

☾

my situation and entire outlook on this planet. is it really that bad? could it be worse? of course it can be, but until you have experienced both, one will never fully grasp the ideas in my head. let alone the one who is thinking them. so i will run until i fall off the face of this earth if i have to, holding onto nothing but a notebook and pen, jotting down every goddamn thing i can so one day it may make sense to someone else. hopefully it can help them and provide a sense of closure to the same answers i seek. if it were not for you, there would be no me. i was created to walk through half of my life alone i believe, in order to acknowledge everyone around me has a specific meaning and task they must complete. today, i will walk with the humans and listen to their voices instead of my own for once.

☾

somewhere down
the unforeseen reality
i am a part of, capsizing
into your soul and completely
submersing my every dream,
thought, and wish is inevitable.
so please, my love, do me a favor,
hold my head under for as long as
you can; killing off any hope for me
to breathe something else again.

☾

my arms found her body and tightly embraced her as if she was an unworldly dream that i never wanted to let go of.
as my mouth opened, this sentence found its way out, "the person standing behind you, will always stand in front when you need them to." it was something i've never said before and i could feel her warm body try and shift around to kiss me. do you know why? because she finally believed in the words someone had told her, just as i will always protect her at all costs.

☾

we then used our hands to

paint the fire that was inside

of us. it was an attempt to create

a beautiful portrait of life and its

magnificent projections of love.

☾

they asked me,
"what does she mean to you?"

i had a smile that could lift the world.
"she means the words i once could not
find, but now are with me every second
of the day. she is my peace, my calm,
and my shelter from the violent storms
i had to endure before on my own.
she means as much to me as the stars
mean to the sky. she is how i find my
way home."

☾

one time, someone told me,
"there is nothing more than love."

bullshit. love every day more than
you did the last. love harder, love
deeper, love as loud as you can.
for the one you are with deserves
your very best not just today, but
the ones that make up an entire
lifetime. you can always do more
than just love.

go beyond that.

and if the heart is what you crave, seek it with all of your love and allow it to consume your soul. if you're not willing to lose it for someone, then why do we try and keep it beating for something we have no idea exists. never forget that we are life and everything consumes one another over time.

all you can ask for
from somebody
is just a chance;

a chance to learn.
a chance to listen.
a chance to love.

having these opportunities,
equals an offer unknown to
most who seek more.

☾

i rolled down my
window and heard
the world speak.

i opened up my
soul and listened
to the universe
explain life to me.

certain conversations
go unnoticed to those
who have a mind
congested with fear.

☾

being alone is just a phrase people use,
because being with someone who is just
a shadow, makes you feel like your bones
got left out in the cold and your heart is
given a chilling reminder that when you
love, you must love from the soul in order
to feel the gravity pull you in, and burn
you with its fierceness.

☾

i told her,

"i am ready to be scared. i need to feel what it's like to touch you and fear what it would be like to lose you. i am ready to live.
i need to experience what being alive feels like while our bodies are entangled between the sheets of our dreams and desires. i am finally ready to open my heart and allow you to see what i've been holding back from others. the love that resides in it has always been too much, always too strong for those who were afraid to feel it. i want my hands to only hold yours and i need my eyes to see you every waking day and every

☾

sleepless night. i am finally ready to give you what i have never shared with anyone before you; my life. my soul. my promises. everything down to the broken pieces of my life i've kept in my pockets, hopelessly trying to put together myself. when i am with you, i am ready for it all: the sensual pain. the overwhelming happiness. the stellar sensation in my bones i get from your fingertips walking down the spine of my back. holding you now, i am willing to love and cherish every naked inch of you until the last breath we share together. then i will continue to search nonstop for you to eternally feel it all over again.

☾

why do you hold me so close?

i do it so i can feel what you

have to say.

she chose the walls she had built over her life to hide behind, instead of giving me a chance to prove to her i was different. i sat there for months, talking to her about life and what she wanted out of it, from the other-side of the stone. i might never get her approval to climb over what she has constructed, but i needed to show her i was willing to listen to her and appreciate a conversation.

even with patience, we do not get everything we want from life.

☾

they found their shadows

under the illuminating moon.

after all this time of searching

for something, they found each

other in the same place they once

lost themselves.

☾

i love how you controlled my eyes without knowing it at all. i understand you couldn't see me looking at you when you would walk away from me, half-naked like a city with a thousand seas. but just know i have never looked away. i will always look at you and stare in amazement, as if we were the first conversations that love talked about before lovers began to stop staring into the eyes that forever held the keys to each other's souls. i have wondered since you finally walked away from me for good, has another man tried to look at you the same? i bet he can't, because my eyes were made for you just as your naked body was meant to be held close to mine. so drown with me in the thousand seas of which you created. loving each other so deeply that we never have to come back up for air.

☾

the way she would carry her broken

wings, made me understand not

everyone you see has to be

perfectly made. they just

need a chance at being

whole again.

we only knew how to live and love one way,
and that was being so caught up in each
other, we forgot humans were created
to have opinions.

☾

today, tomorrow, and the day after that.
two years, five years, and however long
i am alive, i want and need you in my
life.

you, is a place i go often. it is home.
it is in your arms. it is where our lips
meet to tell each other good
morning, i miss you, and
goodnight.

☾

you can never go where your heart
does not lead the way. it goes where
it needs you to go. even if it breaks
in-half, it knows when to sacrifice
itself in order to save you from
the pain.

even if you asked me for
the world, i would hoist it
on my back and bring
it to you.

i will do whatever it takes,
to see you smile again,
my love.

☾

she was kept in the dark
for the majority of her life.

but that didn't stop her from
blooming with love, every day
that she was alive.

all it takes is the light from within,
to exude the most precious of gifts,
created from the darkest of times.

☾

i can still remember the smile you wore when
i told you how captivating and pure you were.

how you were created in the constellations
themselves.

while looking into your eyes that night,
i noticed the stardust that they had left
behind.

(

if i trust you, then it means i am okay with my heart being broken if it should come to that. but now that i am older and on my last breath of love, if you break it, i hope you have already dug the grave to where you can put what's left of a man who always had a hard time trusting himself.

☾

she started crying today, trying to
find comfort in this fucked up
place.

i told her i wrote a poem for her that
would make as a shelter if she
needed somewhere to stay.

safe from all the misery and pain
attaching itself to her face. in this
poem, love will prevail and
restore your faith.

☾

i hope you can find a silver
lining that will propel you
into a positive mindset today
and the future days to come.
just remember to make today
the best day of someone else's
life.

it might turn out to be yours as well.

(

after everything we've been through
and all of the experiences we've taught
each other, please know i am not the only
one who misses you when you are gone.

my heart, body, and soul are all in agreement;
we miss you collectively every time you leave
us in the morning.

☾

may the sun always find you,
even when problems cloud
your day.

even if life is more than you
can handle at times, always
keep in mind someone right
now, somewhere else on this
planet, is having it worse than
you.

☾

for those
individuals
who have
been in my
life and to
the ones that
continue to
leave, you my
love, will always
be the author
of my heart
and i will
continue to
read what you
write for the
rest of my life.

☾

i've read all of the romance books
and watched my share of the classic
kiss me or leave me movies, but at the
end of the day what those things have
in common with how i feel about us
is, that i've always wanted to do more
than just love you.

i want to grow old with you.

☾

life will always present us with challenges
that together we will both face head on.
i know we will always come out of it
stronger than before.

ever since i've met you, i have been falling
in love with you, one "i love you" at a time.

☾

we started this thing a while
back with no rules or promises,
but i need you to understand it
will always be me and you.

for no other reason than our souls
met and spoke the same language;
love.

if that can be enough for you,
i swear it will always be enough
for me.

☾

once there was a time where i played your heart strings and made my song come alive. we both conducted our music to the sound of our heart beats. but now we listen to a different beat.
our music still plays loud through the walls of a renovated love song; echoing through the halls as it spills out into the streets. it plays to when i saw you and you saw me. the hollowness of was once my soul, is now filled with music from another girl. instead of just a single heart string, we now play as a symphony, conducted by our broken dreams.

sometimes all it takes is,

one smile.

one look.

one kiss.

one moment shared together.

it's the unknown that makes them whole.

☾

make today the

day you have been

waiting for your whole life.

☾

there are only three
things that matter
in this world:

your love for me.
my love for you.
our love forever.

☾

you embody everything
that is good in this world.
the purest form of sincere
and beauty.

without question, you are
my clarity.

☾

there is not enough space on this page to explain what you mean to me. i write in a way that only you and i understand, and i love that about us. if i could, i would write out each meaning to you for all of the writings i have made for you. i love how you smile and i can feel it through your words. i love how we laugh at the most random things and we have a kind of sarcasm that it takes to understand each other. i may not be able to write each meaning, but i only need one definition, and that is you. you are the blood of my words. they embody everything i hope to do with you one day.
you are so much more than what i ever thought anyone could mean to me. i tell you all the time just how special you are, because deep down in my soul, it knows it too. whenever i think about you, my heart races faster and my hands search

☾

for your body. i write for you and about you, because i love you. this is more than a paragraph and all the words and letters combined could never add up to, or equal the love i have for you in my heart. hopefully this will allow you to understand why i write for you with such passion, drive, and focus. you are always near me and i feel you all around me during my days and nights. now that you are to this portion of the page, i just wanted to tell you how much i truly care for you and i hope your day is as golden as your heart. thank you for being here for me and for understanding me and my words. they are to you, for you, and about you. i cannot express that enough and as hard as i try, i am still trying and learning new ways to tell you and show i love you.

☾

my story is complex, though i am just a simple man trying to convey what i feel. a broken home molded my soul into what it is today. without tragedy in my life, i would not understand the meaning of struggle. i have spent many years of waking up in cold sweats, scared of not just my nightmares, but the fact that i may not live long enough to give all of me to this universe that had created me. sometimes i feel like i was made with the leftover parts of scattered and broken hearts that make up this wonderful world in which we live. i feel so much pain at times and suffering through the vibes of others that it is completely overwhelming for me to do a simple task like closing my eyes.

(

but i know once i wake up it is a new day to give back to those that have given me more than i could've ever ask for; a chance, an opportunity, and a new life. one that is not just living, but one that feels so deeply and passionate about writing that i literally almost write down every word and thought that comes through my bones and lands in my soul. creating life on a page and giving a voice to those who might just need that extra ounce of hope. here's to all those that are broken. together in time, we will all become whole again.

we were just two star crossed
lovers, meeting across the distant
sky; hoping for a shooting star to
help us take flight. she had eyes
like diamonds, the brightest ones
the universe had ever seen.

we made love on a blanket
of stars, tumbling through
the galaxies.

☾

as i got into my truck and started to drive,
i was trying to make all of my words make
sense to you tonight. so much to say and
so much to do, hoping love will come with
me for the ride so i can tell you, love is
this way. as i pull into your drive, and step
out of my truck, i feel the rain fall on my face
and it washes my nerves away, but it can't cool
the fire burning inside of me. i sat there for a
while and soaked it all in. as i walked to your
door, i took a second longer, and then took
some more. i thought to myself, "i can tell you
all the reasons why i love you and why i took this
long drive. i can look into your eyes and without
saying a word, i can feel the love for me inside
you. with you touching me, you have reached
for my soul, so before we run away, follow me,

☾

because love is this way." as i began to knock on your door, my heart fell to the floor, and i reached down inside of me and pulled it back up the same way you helped me change my life and gave me your love. you opened the door and i saw your smile. without any hesitation, i wrapped you in my arms and stayed like that until our eyes were dry.
with the rain falling down and the night air getting cold, you grabbed for my hand as i gave you my coat. we got through talking outside and headed in the house to get lost together by the fire. then and there i was amazed by everything that could happen to us in the following days. with you looking at me and me looking at you, i couldn't help but tell

☾

you that i decided to drive all this way, through the day and night to tell you, i need you now. i look into your eyes and without you saying a word, i felt the love from you for me deep down inside. with you touching me and me touching you, we touched each others soul. now all that's left to do is walk through the rain and let it fall from our face. so follow me, because i love you is this way.

☾

i want to
travel the
world and
write as if
i would
never die.
that my
words
will escape
the grave
and just
take my
body when
it is time.

☾

i was falling apart at the seams,
but you sewed me back together,
piece by piece.

your hands worked like angel's wings.
careful and precise, you made me whole
again and brought me back to life.

so here i stand, saved by an amazing
grace, thanking you for loving a
broken man in a wretched
place.

(

it is amazing how much
one human can miss the
other. when all it took was
to hear the sound of their
voice to fall in love.

she whispers in my ear every
night,

"i love you, forever and always."

☾

i saw you sitting alone on the bench by the tree with yellow leaves falling from it. i thought, "is she alone on purpose, or is she waiting for someone?" after ten minutes or so, i slowly got up and walked over and then passed you.
i didn't know if i had the courage or the gumption to say hello to such a beautiful human. i continued down to an empty bench, three benches down from you. i looked at my watch, that damn thing was moving slower than i just walked. i told myself, "if you do not talk to her now, you will regret this for the rest of your life." i attempted to walk over to you, but my knees were knocking together so loud, i am surprised you didn't hear me approaching. i finally got the

☾

word "hello" out of my mouth and with great joy you said, "good morning." but the way you said it, had my butterflies chasing each other, looking for its soul-mate. i asked you, "can i sit down or are you waiting for someone?" you said, "not waiting at all, just admiring the leaves and their colors. i love watching them fall." i thought about it before i said it and what repercussions would come with a "no." i asked her, "can i sit down?" she laughed and said, "why of course you can. i would love the company. it gets lonely on these benches. the wood itself feels hollow." we talked for about an hour and then we went to get coffee. she got a latte and i got a cup of the special blend they had roasting in the back. together we made up our own random conversations; the ones where you feel so comfortable that you forget three hours have passed and your cheeks hurt from laughing so much. we finished two cups of coffee each and we exchanged numbers. but she drew a falling leave on the paper she gave to me. i still keep it to this day, behind the picture of you and me. alone we sat, transcending what makes life the most random of things. you never know how your day will turn out, just like a leave won't ever know how falling from a tree could make the beginnings of a glorious and ever lasting love between two complete strangers on a cold september morning.

☾

she asked me,
"why do you love me?"

i answered, "i love you because you love me. i love how you let your hair down when you come home. i love our random conversations at 3am. i love you for seeing all of my faults and scars, yet you love me as if i am perfect. you are the reason love was created. you project everything it entails. i love you is a phrase used to describe a feeling, a sensation unknown to those who are scared of giving away pieces of their life."

to me, she has recovered those pieces of mine and put me back together, lovingly.

(

after burning the food that she was trying to cook for us, she said, "i am sorry. i tried not to ruin it this time." i laughed like i always do, and said, "even if all else fails, i'll always love you, because you try your damnedest to make everything perfect and it reminds me of why i fell in love with you the first time. you never give up."

(

a long week out of town finally ended and i came home to her trying to make the perfect dinner for us. i quietly approached her, just soft enough on my feet where she got startled by merely my touch. there she was, trying again to impress me with this meal for kings, when all i needed was just her. i was hungry for love and hungry just to hold her again after being gone. never forget why you fell in love in the first place. that way, you won't ever misplace it.

(

i told her, "i love you."

she said, "i love you too, babe."

i then asked her, "where would you like to live?" she replied by saying, "maybe california. i heard the beaches are beautiful." with that, i already knew what i was going to say next. "we will live wherever you choose, but for right now, you are living in my heart. you are my heartbeat and my love supply." love will follow you wherever you lead it. take it wherever you go when you leave. it is a gift that most people will never see.

☾

she said, "where do you go, when things just go to shit?" i looked at her, hiding my laugh inside, because she hardly ever curses. i said, "i go to the memory of us meeting." that night,
i decided to go out and take a chance on life itself. something told me to dress accordingly, because first impressions are key. i decided to have a drink at this rundown, hole in the wall bar named "the getaway." i asked her, "do you remember that place?" she laughed hysterically, and said, "yes! yes i do!" then i asked her, "what has you so bent out of shape, sweetheart?" she looked at me as if she had developed memory loss in a matter of seconds, "i am not sure."
with a wild smile, i said, "you're welcome.
told you it works, babe." when trying to forget the worst day of your life, always remember the best day. it allows perspective to creep in and tell you, it's not that bad.

☾

love has to be reciprocal. it cannot work with someone trying to make up the other half of a love that does not exist. no matter how loud your love is for the other, it is best to go your separate ways if what you say is different from what you mean. forever is a long time to love, but suffering lasts a lifetime.

☾

she came home with this look on her face and i asked her, "darling, what is wrong?" she said, "it is life. i am tired of trying. especially when all it does is make me cry." so i pulled her in as tight as i could, and told her, "listen to me. those people don't know what kind of a soul you love with. they don't know how that smile makes my day nor will they ever know how big your heart is, because you have had to put up with me your whole life. even though everything is going well, it doesn't mean that it is going right. i will always be there for you to help you laugh and to help you smile. that is what i found sexy about you in the first place. so there is no reason to cry."

☾

she said, "your heart is beautiful." i have never heard that before, but it made my soul smile. so i told her, "what's mine is yours." she began to tear up, because nobody had ever given their heart to her." love is a lot of things, but to me, love is about giving your everything in order to make what you want become reality. even if you have to sacrifice in the long run. love is not about doing the necessary because you have to. love is about doing the extraordinary, rearranging the idea that love is supposed to be defined already. make it your own. allow the soul to speak the words that your heart is too scared to say.

i love you is not just a saying. it is a way of life.

☾

she said, "i want to be more than just
married to the thought of you. i need
all of you; your body, heart and soul."
i told her, "i will be there and give you
whatever you need. because without
you, i am a captain who is steering his
boat into the black sea of forever;
where there is no turning around,
only washing ashore to be lost and
never found. my desire for you is
something that chaos only dreams
about. you are my beacon of love
and hope, guiding me back home.

☾

she said, "i come with a lot of baggage."
i told her, "i have been carrying mine
longer than i care to remember, but
i will promise to help you carry yours
however far you need me to." in times
of bringing up the past and trying to move
forward with your life, you will have to accept
the fact that baggage will come with anyone
you meet. life is a journey that doesn't prepare
us for what we need. we have to experience life
for what it is; failed relationships, death, love,
and all the memories that haunt each one of us.
for me, i am willing to help and will always be.
that is who i am. do not apologize to me for
baggage that has accumulated over the years.
like i said, i come with more than enough.

☾

last night, as we looked up at the sky,
i asked you, "how many stars can you see?"
you told me, "i am not sure. billions if
i had to guess." you then asked me, "how
about you?" i leaned over and whispered
in your ear, "i only see two." the glow in your
eyes is something that the stars wish they had,
but they cannot have them or you. you are mine
to look at and admire. wherever this leads,
i know i am in it for the long haul; bumps and
detours included. however long it takes to feel
the love that you have given to me, i will be
right by your side. making sure that glow never
fades from your eyes.

☾

our love will be poetry made between the sheets. where two bodies rage out of control for hours in a sexual daze. hydrating on the sweat that pours from your body, i will drink you dry and make you come to life. with your eyes looking into mine, we will make love feel like a sensual design. manipulated by two souls longing to know what it is like to touch heaven.

(

she said, "promises are made to be broken."
i told her, "if you are the promise someone
needs then you will never break it or their
heart." people make promises all the time,
knowingly accepting the fact that they might
not be able to complete the entire process.
for some, it is a challenge in itself, creating false
hope for the ones they love. all i have to say to
those who think that promises are made to be
broken is, you have never loved someone
the way i love her. my promise to her is, i will
keep her in my heart forever. if something
should happen, i hope my heart breaks first.

☾

she asked, "does my makeup look okay?
is the outfit alright?" i simply said without
hesitation, "your face is angelic. it's perfect
without the makeup. the outfit wraps you as
well as my hands would if i had to cover your
naked body." time and time again, she goes
out looking like the heavens made her a
perfect ten. the truth of the matter is, in my
eyes, she is perfect. she is my ten all of the
time. without the makeup and outfit, i awake
to the definition of beauty every morning.
it allows me to be thankful that someone like
her exists, to cover up and hide all the mistakes
and wrongs i have done in my life.

☾

the life and times of two individuals still
trying to search and locate themselves
in a crowded room, full of heartache
and misdirection.

where a wrong turn or a false step leads to
doom. i must say though, she has me all
kinds of distracted and confused.

☾

it is not every day you stumble upon fate's

doorstep and it lets you in. somehow, i even

forgot to knock and she let me in anyway.

now she has me in every room of the house,

deciding where we should sleep.

☾

i have come to terms with the fact that i might be alone for the rest of my life, but i will continue to write as if i am madly in love with the universe; falling for it every single night.

i have seen first hand the power it carry when we are able to read in-between the lines. if there is one thing that i ask from you, it is to fall in love with everything you fucking do. even if you have to marry the idea that it will eventually get better.

allow it to manifest into your wildest dreams. then when you are ready, attack it with all your soul, and reality will become everything you see and know.

as the angels gathered around they said,
"let's give them one more chance. love is
a precious thing and to have it once is hard
to find. it was the star's fault that love escaped
them the first time." as they continued on, one
of them said, "i know they still love each other.
i hear them talking about one another all the
time to themselves. i even see part of their
dreams when they think nobody is watching."
after a long discussion, they all went to find the
twin flames they had been ordered to reunite.
off they went, in search of a second chance.
"however long it takes, even if another angel
takes my place, we will make things right."

they all told
me that she
was dead to
the world.
well, you all
are the ones
who are lifeless.
for she comes
alive during the
night time,
when everyone
else dreams of
finding
something to
live for.

i tend to talk to myself to see if i will answer. then out of nowhere, my thoughts begin to shout onto paper. it's still unclear to me how overpowering they can be. armed with just a pen, i take over and start writing again. listening to what they scream at me, i continue writing down lost memories. they begin to flow like the ocean is flooding with drifters, made out to be lost writings i thought would eventually sink. instead, they float along in my mind, without an anchor or a single lifeline. down the sea they go, like messages in a bottle, filled with hope.

and then she smiled.

within that exact moment in time, she did everything that everyone told her she wouldn't be able to do in life. with a little help from her soul, she gathered up the parts that were broken and forged a meaning that others would never get to know. she finally started living for herself and against all odds, this woman, this pearl of a spirit, conquered and defeated all of the odds. she was ultimately set free to dance among those who had always crippled her mind to the concept that following others was the meaning of life. now she dances within the kisses of the moon;
slowly becoming the waves of the night
that now crash over me and you.

i write as if my heart

could sing a love song.

as if my eyes could sing

a sad song. as if my mind

could sing along to both.

i am the lonely performer

onstage, waiting for the

crowd to enter through

the gates.

)

why does the rain make feel as if heaven is
crying again? it sometimes makes me want
to go out and shower in the angels' tears;

trying to save them from falling to this
unforgiving place.

to me, being broken is what
life is all about. it takes being
broken to find the one you
need to put you back
together.

in the end, you are both
creating something new
and original.

as a kid, i had so many thoughts
in my head, i thought i was
different, until i discovered
a way to bring life to
paper, with just a
pen.

you see, now all of my runaway
thoughts and colliding words,
have a place to live. time has
passed and i have grown
older, my thoughts are
now my children in a
sense.

i've seen them grow and mature
as well in place where i thought
i was different.

☽

we all have our moments where it
is just us and the universe, to do as
we wish. for instance, you kissing
the moon goodnight and singing
the falling stars a lullaby.

you sing, "oh falling star, why do
you fall so hard? oh falling star,
may i make a wish with you
tonight? promise me you will
grant me the wish to have
sweet serenity and a life
filled with bliss."

to me, you are more beautiful than
any glorious dream i could envision.
you are my dream within a dream
i hope to never wake up from.

i will never give up on you. for they discover

new galaxies every day. you could become a

whole new world once you start to believe

in yourself. life is about finding out who

you are on the inside. it is not about

others who judge what they cannot see.

seeing you again

will be something

my dreams won't

even be able to

accommodate.

)

her morning kisses were the reason the sun

could never stay gone. every day, he would

rise again to taste the sweetness of her

song. she sang for him and for him

alone.

if i could put music to my words, would you sing it to me? every high note and run, please do this for me, my love. i need to have your voice to keep these pages alive. they need your soothing tone that you were born with. it would provide the words a dance floor for those who are alone and needing a hand. one that would take them to a place where strangers become friends and drug addicts can find the peace they have longed searched for. a place where orphans become loved and the hooker on the street can find peace within a soft and gentle hug. where deadbeats like me, can find a drink without having to drown in sorrow and guilt. a place for castaways that never had a choice but to leave. for those like me who still search for someone that believes we all deserve an opportunity. help me, please, sing a song that is written by a lost soul who loves you. without you, my words are falling stars, crashing to earth without a fucking chance to survive. if you sing, i will sing. then who knows, we might just all sing together. a perfect harmony, sung by the world's greatest symphony; love.

she understood the toughest part about becoming herself was ultimately letting go of the things she thought she could never live without. she's laughing now without their consent and she's okay with how it feels for the first time. it's something she could get used to. it's astonishing what can happen when you replace empty things with handpicked happiness. one can never grab enough and the feeling is unmistakable, like the ten minutes before you get home after being gone for too long. there's no more worry inhabiting her eyes and the sadness creeping down her cheeks has dried. a new foundation has been built on top of her porcelain dreams. under her skin are feathers and ashes resembling pride which is still alive. she knows what it took to get to this unmarked page of her life and she will continue creating new space for the things she loves. you never understand the significance of absence, until you leave yourself, thinking you will return the same.

there's a ghost in the back of my throat and my skin doesn't fit anymore. i was wondering how long it would take for me to grow out of my bones and when the old me would finally leave. sometimes we get too comfortable with ourselves to ever look for a change. we think change will somehow discover us and we grow back into being satisfied again. life is tricky, weird, strange, and downright unforgiving, but it has the capability of blowing our messy and complicated minds with something so absurdly beautiful, it knocks the rust off of our souls. it happened to me about two years ago, and the water i find myself looking out into has never reflected a purer image. don't settle for the shallows when the uncertainty lies in the depths. that's where you find the realness of life. that's where you find your guts. that' where you find the truth you've been to afraid to say. reality isn't for everyone, but it is fair to those who are honest with themselves.

when we shared

our stories about

the type of pain

love can bring,

i knew i would

never hurt again.

you must be willing to stretch your limits if you want her. you must be agile with every step you take. when she is ready, she will let you know, but not a second sooner. there's beauty in her approach to life, and i will admit, i am ready to fall off the edges surrounding her, just to feel that second of meaning.

)

i found myself today, trying to come up with a word to describe what you mean to me. in that same moment, i tried to formulate a thought that could describe what i am feeling for you. after several minutes of contemplating ideas, i came to the abrupt conclusion that all i could or ever will be able to use to explain, is your name. there are other places i could go and other people that i could meet, but i found you, and having you like this, is and will always be better than having anything else with someone besides you. you are my uncontrollable sensation i hope never ends. you're it for me

)

and because of that, i live knowing the possibility of being with you surpasses all logic and reason to ever try to begin without you. we are only here for so long and then we return to the stars, but once you find your 11:11, your heart will never forget the time and location of the other. with a single thought, i changed how the world turned for me, and now your precious name is pressed against a lover who says, "i believe you" and means it. sweet one, you will forever live on my lips and i will speak to you gently and with purpose so you can feel how much love resides in a name.

❯

her intent isn't malicious, but do not give her a reason to be. some say she comes across as being callous, but she's as durable as any structure still standing after the storm. she will use all of her powers to disassociate herself from people who misuse her energy. she is a formidable force that will protect her heart from those thinking they can borrow it for a little while. it's not a temporary home. it is a paradise for the one who treats her with the respect she has earned. give her that and she will give you a friend and lover who will stay true as long as you

)

fight for her when she can't find the words to say. she's the breath you forgot to take when you thought you were okay. though she can be anxious at times, worried about if she's living life to the fullest, there's no other person you'd want in your corner when the bell rings. some will remove themselves from the situation, but she will always stand up for the people she loves. you can tell by the way the sun rests on her shoulders she's made differently.

as we bathe
together with
the silence
surrounding
us, the breaths
we take tell a
story of a
moment shared
between two
endearing
souls.

this hunger i have for you cannot be
controlled by just a simple taste of
you. i am going to need all of you:

your lips. your neck. your shoulders.
your thighs. your skin pressing against
mine. your eyes looking at me, while we
both watch my hands walk across your
body, as they inch closer to every spot
that burns for more.

☽

this morning, i had an immense urge to hug the sun, as i tried to feel its infinite warmth before i got out of bed. so i made sure to roll over and put my arms around you, even though i knew you were still dreaming.

the undying truth is, i absolutely hate not being close to you. there is something beautiful about holding each other in the morning that awakes our souls and turns them into animals who are starving for a taste of flesh; a carnal uproar there have been so many lonely nights in my life, but now your comely body is next to mine and all i want to do is close my tranquil eyes with you, until your sensual whispers wake me in the morning. together we shall feast on love and each other's company by consuming voracious kisses and insatiable touching that always leads us to an uncontrollable desire full of perpetual jonesing for more.

☽

i could write a thousand lines about how
goddamn beautiful and sexy you are and
how you tickle my wolfish soul with your
devilish tongue, but i need you to know it
is more than just that. i write because i love
you and you are my inspiration when all i
needed was someone to dream with.

you're more than just words on a page, baby.
you are the absolute reasoning behind why i
now write the way i do.

☽

i fucked up.
i never once thought about a future, because i never saw myself seeing the day where i lived to tell about it. i don't have a 401k. i don't have any bonds or stocks i can fall back on. i live my life for one day only and that is today. when i was younger, it was about living fast and reckless. be as spontaneous as i could; never thinking about the result or outcome. i lived with no intentions of ever regretting my past, only learning from it if i ever got the chance to see the next day. i've had several "next days" and it's hard, well, fucking excruciating knowing what i should've done so i wouldn't be where i am at right now. i'm not lost. i'm just in the wind, and my compass seems to spin sporadically around the sun. if you are fighting more than you can withstand, open your eyes and throw every goddamn thing you can at it.

☽

i've got south carolina on my mind.

oh, how i miss the way you brought

life to the lonely; strolling your sands

at night. the smell of the sea breathed

new life into me. i hope to see you soon.

until then, i will continue wishing you the

moon.

☽

the only algorithm

i ever needed to

learn, was that you

plus me would always

equal a life together

that extended into

the far reaching spaces

between the stars.

)

one of the most intense moments
of my life was when i missed you,
without ever meeting you.

the universe would often speak about
you in my dreams. so when it granted
me the honor of bringing us
together, you told me about your
vision and how our two worlds had
collided.

i am very thankful for the madness.

i have always valued her touch more
than any woman i had ever held
before. when we were older,
living in the twilight of our
years, i told her,

"thank you for never letting go of my
heart and for leaving your fingerprints
all over my soul. without you, i would
just be another man with a first and last
name. you made me someone who gave
a damn about living for others as well as
for myself. when it is my time to go, you
will always be able to find me. follow the
fingerprints i leave behind. they have
always belonged to you."

having the chance to finally

fall in love with you every day,

over and over again, would be

the equivalent of the sun and

moon experiencing eternity

together.

when it came time
to open our hearts
at night, i fell in love
with her every single
time.

for it was the warmth
i desperately needed
to stay alive.

)

over the years i have lost so many great friends.

the tears that i've cried since, are a reminder to

me to give all i have to this day that's been

presented. hopefully they are smiling down

at me and helping me guide this pen.

as she let her hair down, my heart fell to
the floor. how could something so simple
as being yourself, make me fall for you
every time you walk through the door?

a question i hope that's never answered,
but only repeated to myself about her
for the rest of my life.

"only time will tell."

that's what everyone likes to believe.
though tonight, being with you under
the twilight of night and the moon
slowly approaching its climax,
is where i was meant to be.

perfection captured by two souls living
in the theater of the universe.

spinning you around on the dance floor has
me dancing with love. the look in your eyes
when you come back around full circle is the
only satisfaction i will ever need. it was if i had
died right there in the middle of your arms.
i closed my eyes and saw your soul bursting
through your skin, begging me to hold you
while the band kept playing our favorite
song.

all we need is a handful
of each other's soul to
hold onto while trying
to travel the galaxies
surrounding our
lives.

)

she was the flesh to my bones;
covering every inch of my
troubled soul.

allowing me the opportunity
to see what life could be like
feeling alive, while trying
to exist in a world where
promises do not match
the heart in which they
are kept in.

don't you get it, while you stay out
until the early hours of the morning,
drinking away time itself, she patiently
waits for you to be drinking her in with
every waking moment spent trying to
become the magic she so desperately
needs.

☽

she wanted a life together, but more
importantly, she needed love in the
most purest of forms.

i gathered up all of my strength and
courage i could muster, showing her
my scars from past mistakes that
marked my life.

i allowed her to see my open flesh,
all the way down to the bones
where my pain is buried.

tie me with your ropes of lust.
knot them with your soulful
kisses and take my heart
hostage if you must.

for tonight, there will be a universal
domination of stars; colliding to
become a supernova of love.

i will never be afraid of any man walking this earth. i have passed through hell without catching fire and looked the devil straight in his eyes; making him the one to blink first.

now i am finally climbing out of the ash and rubble below me, trying to stand with my past beneath my feet, while stepping on the throat of the old me; killing off any remnants that tried to follow me to where i am now.

all i need is a hand to help me for the final step of making my journey complete.

)

last night i reached for your hand,

but you allowed me to grab your

heart.

only then did i know what it was like

to be seen by hope and to be held

by the moon.

when you catch me looking at the
stars, just know i am relishing in
the fact that they allowed me
to have someone like you.

when wishes are made, they sacrifice
their lives in order to create living
dreams for those who need
them. i only have one
question for you,
my dear,

"how long had you been listening to me
up there?"

)

i've fallen in love with you every day since we have met. it is a constant cycle of emotions i experience through the entire span of one day that is filled with overwhelming support from you.

that's what love is, the act of falling over
and over again for the same person for
the rest of your life together, making
sure to never become complacent
with what life has given you.

believing takes two;
you and your soul.

when in doubt, the soul
stays strong because it
has seen you overcome
so much more.

if you looked into my eyes deep enough,
you would finally see heaven and hell.
where angels and demons battle each
other for the right to see the world as
anything but normal.

do not stare too long, they have been
known to scare others away that do
not have the courage to stay by my
side.

then again, that's just life.

another 4am conversation leads to us talking
about the universe and all that has yet to be
explored in our lives.

we must be extremely bored or so in love
with each other we do not mind missing
the rest of what our bodies need.

we looked at each other with a certain
glaze of forever in our eyes, and then
we both said, "can we stay awake a
little longer?"

the sun is almost up and i want the
nighttime to have all that's left of
you and i right now.

)

life is about the moments in-between breaths

and complete silence, where the only thing

needed is a beating heart resonating

through the depths of your soul.

)

i have been writing for what seems like
a thousand years now. i think i've become
a part of this chair, as i now glide to where
i go instead of walking to my next destination.
i will not allow myself a break until i have
described the perfect way of how you make
me feel. with my back tied with knots of pain
and my neck as stiff as yesterday's thoughts,
i will tell you that i never thought i could love
anyone more than i loved the person i was
trying to be. you might think that is arrogant or

☽

conceited to say, but to live and grow up in a home where i had to love myself more is something i have yet to tell anyone. growing up, i was a kid trying to find love from someone who gave a damn. it seemed as if i was the only one who ever did. so for me to tell you that, is me saying i will never love anyone else as much as i love you. a promise my soul will hold onto as it leaves this universe to find you again when it is my time to patiently wait for you, my dear. goodnight, my love, and i will see you in about five minutes.

i constantly find myself
during the day, thinking
about a woman i have
never met before in my
life. she is taking up all
of my time and memory
that i thought could
never be used for just
one human. i hope one
day to meet her and
find out if the universe
truly does bring stars
together to form a
dream.

i loved you for who you wanted to be. for there was never nor will there ever be a judgmental bone placed in my body.

you are you.

to me, it will always depict the love for us. nothing more is needed for you and i to venture into forever.

)

have you ever just took the time
to stand quietly still, with your
busy eyes closed and peacefully
breathed in the universe and
the surrounding moments that
life has brought you?

always believe that your
dreams will come to
fruition.

for at one point in our lives,
we too were just dreams.

allow them to become
a beautiful form of
reality that spreads
throughout a
million lifetimes.

)

always stay young within the lines of reality.
life will blind you with unforgiving words
and haunting thoughts that will become
toxic if you continue to drink the poison
it leaves behind.

not only

can my

demons

swim,

they can

drink just

like me.

i hear voices that
are not my own.
i see shadows that
do not belong to me.

why must my mind be
constantly wandering
around drunk and
stumbling over
everyone else's
thoughts?

i will always be thankful for
our paths crossing when
they did.

you allowed me a chance to
finally look within my soul to
see something that you knew
had been there when you first
met me;

a second chance at life,
love, and true happiness.

we drew a heart in the sand with our names in
the middle. there was a line already dividing
the sea and the shore, but you told me to
take your hand and trust you that it would
be okay to love again. so i did.

we swam in the fears of our past and made
love to the idea of something more profound
happening, as the skies over the water brought
us thunder and lightning to showcase our souls.

i want to catch the moment
that passed you by so you
and i could get lost in it.

let's create sandcastles and
call them a second chance.

)

she never needed much in life,
because she was happy without
the white picket fence everyone
dreamed about.

the garden of stars in her backyard
would always be more than enough.

you can still visit and watch her
wishes become beautiful and
true.

i loved how when we would have to stop
holding hands that we never really let go
at all.

we stay connected at the soul wherever
this wild and crazy world takes us.

always hydrate on
love and your soul
will never be thirsty
for anything else in
this world or the
next.

she was the combination of all
the fantasies and dreams i've
ever experienced or wanted
in my life.

she was a walking wildfire of flowers
dancing in an open field, longing
to be held just right.

it was the chaos created by our storms
that allowed us a chance to dance with
the drops of rain falling from our hearts.

now we are growing our own garden of
adventures, and i cannot wait for them
to bloom.

)

out of all the things in the world, her most favorite item she owned did not hang in a closet or get lost in her dresser drawers. she kept it in a picture frame her mother made with wood from the barn they used to play in when she was younger.

it is a letter that reads,

"when you are ready to become more than what you thought you could be, always live there and never leave. one idea is born from a thought that then matures into an action. never stop finding yourself."

she not only became more, she loved more as well.

be still long enough to appreciate her love. always listen to her before you think you know what she wants. never allow her to think that she is just beautiful, because she is everything the sun and moon worships. continue to give her all the roses you can, because one day you'll learn the hard way once she lets go of your hand for another man that can do all of this for her.

she never had to beg me for anything.

all she simply had to do was look at me

and bite her lower lip. within those few

moments, my mind had played out

the entire day with her and i knew the

clothes we were wearing would not be

a part of the plan.

☽

can you stay awake a
little longer, my dear?

i need to see love before
i fall asleep.

please keep your eyes
on me, my dear.

i want to watch the angels
dance around the moons
before they get any
closer to you.

when she was younger, she would swim in the waters back behind her home. it was an enchanting dream because of the way the moon played with the waves crashing into her. when she was little, there was never an adventure she wouldn't chase down to be a part of. now that she has matured and grown into her soul, she understands those moments a little clearer. she knows who she is and what she wants, and believe me, there is nothing more unstoppable in the universe than a woman who knows that. she will pick stars from the sky to make it believable. the child she was back then still lives inside of her, so whenever she gets a chance, she goes back to those same shores to hear the waves calling for her to help them with the tides again. once you leave a place like that, the moon knows its children, and greets her with each splash of light.

one of the things i love
the most is, when her
cold toes go in
search to find
the warmth
of mine.

it is all about the soulful sensation
she gives to me, whether it's by
her touch, scent, or the way
her eyes tell me to come
closer.

i know when it is time to get up, she
will go over to my drawer and pull out
a pair of my socks, but i have already
laid out a pair for her when she was
too cold to move. they look better
on her angel feet anyway.

)

i guess you could
say that i finally
stopped allowing
you to use my
backbone as a
leaning post.

)

i feel sorry for you. how can you not love her for everything she wants to be. she is trying her hardest to please you and you just sit there with this look on your face that says, "not interested today." well, how about if i told you i was. i am always interested in those who have fought through the fire and came out the other-side reborn and unafraid. all she wanted was to be appreciated, but then again, not everyone sees value in things they don’t understand.

she did not need to hear another
excuse. all she needed in life was
love and the honest truth.

make her smile, make her laugh,
and dammit, never make her cry.

love every single part of her body
and always show her what she has
dreamed about; a beautiful life.

i was born a human,
but i will live and love
while walking this earth,
understanding that i will
die a hopeful soul.

it was all in the way she could love
and heal the broken. she still puts
back together the fragmented
pieces of the stars that fall
every night in order to
be closer to her.

i've never seen anyone hold something
so gentle with the precise amount of
care needed to make a beautiful
thing, transform into what it
needed to be.

i just want to live in a place where hearts are able to hold the broken souls, instead of experiencing a life that shackles our minds with a paralyzing agent mixed with negativity and fear, called society. somehow, it continues to force itself down our throats and we just sit there, dying from the lies and suffocation of a world full of jagged edges that tear and rip ideas and voices from those who were born to speak their mind.

i am an uncommon soul born from the darkness inside imprisoned walls. i am dust from another place where love was a cure for all.

i have lived. i have died.

i have seen life on both sides, and yet,
we continually fight without
understanding why.

she was always searching for something more,

so i gave her the space needed in order to find

it. i am now in-between dreams, hoping to

finally awake to feel her answer.

as he was opening the car door
to let her out, she looked at him
and asked, "where is the one place
you want to go that you have not
been?"

taken aback by how random the
question was, he smiled and
told her, "your heart."

he then kissed her softly, and said,
"goodnight, sweet one."

one evening, we were sitting across from one another enjoying our dessert. i was on my last piece of tiramisu and she was finishing off her strawberry ice cream.

in that split second, as i saw her tongue glide over her lips, i could taste everything that life could be.

life is a funny thing sometimes. there will always be people who will stay happy for you and be there for you no matter what.

those friends are hard to find. the other kind will say they are happy for you and once you have a little bit of success, they stop talking to you and completely drop out of your life. i say to those people, "you were never really a part of my life to begin with and i am glad you are no longer here as a friend."

it gives meaning and makes me appreciate the ones who never left when i gave them plenty of reasons to leave.

thinking about something you already know

the answer to, is best for both parties if you

just say the simple truth. there's no reason

to complicate it. life does a great job of

that already.

-love-

a feeling that gets
misunderstood
because of the
context in which
it is used.

the way to the heart
and the reason for a
dying soul.

☽

would one night be enough if you could never have a life together? or would you chance it and risk your heart for the sake of getting to feel her breathe and feeling her touch for the rest of your life?

)

and i will love her for the truth i see in her eyes. we all make mistakes and second chances are not given out to everyone. holding each other's hand, we walked though this broken and divided world, ceaselessly trying to leave love's mark on everything that has been stamped "fragile." including our own delicate hearts, which were always held the wrong way by the ones before us.

today is long enough to
create an entire lifetime
of memories. close your
eyes with me and put
your hands in mine,
so that we can start
building together.

i held her defeated and frail soul tightly in my arms; providing the shelter it desperately needed in order to finally rest.

then i went to war with those who caused her to lose not only her smile, but the hope she once carried within her.

)

she had those champagne colored eyes with lips
that had been kissed by merlot. a soul that had
been dipped in whiskey and a rose for a tongue.
over the years she'd become everything
that she had ever loved. i was one of the lucky
ones that knew her, even though we would
never be more than friends, it was just a gift
to be in her presence. last night, we got drunk
off life and it will always be an adventure when
you have sin on your side.

)

life will always be complicated, but we tried

to simplify things as much as possible by

exchanging words for touch. our world was

a place in which we had no rules or safe words

to worry about. it was just us creating a fire with

fingertips, lips, and a passion unknown to those

who are scared of getting burned.

☽

i'll never stop touching, holding, or kissing your body as long as i am awake. even if i have to close my eyes, my arms will always be around you.

when morning comes, i will never have to know what missing you feels like.

)

today, i was eating lunch in portland, tx. which is five minutes away from where i live. quite frankly, it had been one of those days where i didn't need a calendar to know it was monday. it had been a pretty long day up until that point, with the weather showcasing my mood at the time; cloudy with a slight breeze containing an uncertain outlook. as i finished my meal, a mother and daughter were in front of me, walking out the door. the child, who was handicapped, held onto her mother's right arm, as she could barely walk for herself and the mom was carrying the lunch they couldn't finish in her left hand. she looked behind her shoulder to see me and without any hesitation, held the door open for me with her left elbow. as i got outside i thanked her and the

daughter had this smile that made me tear up,
just as i am doing now writing this. i thought to
myself at that moment, "what the fuck is wrong
with you, zac? you have your health, all of your
limbs, and a mind that still functions properly.
appreciate what you have and don't let the
unknown future allow you to over-analyze
everything to make it worse than what it
actually is. you have a great life, so live it
instead of worrying all the damn time."
thank you to the single mother and her
beautiful daughter for showing me that
today and every day, we have the power
to make the sun appear whenever we need
hope; it lives in us all.

she might have lost a glass slipper and missed out on the kiss, but she's not complaining about it. there's too much life to live and worrying about what could've been doesn't cause her to lose sleep anymore. there will be another time and place for the one she's after, but right now, it's about making sure her own cup is filled by herself daily. there is no other kind of remedy for healing like self-love. when the pain is begging for you to feel it, you must acknowledge it, because inside is a cure you are searching for. she speaks a certain way that causes others to flinch and she giggles at the mere fact that cussing is frowned upon if you're a woman. a few choice words may exit her mouth, but believe me, she's thought about every single one before speaking, and is just fine whether or not you accept it. she has a middle finger if you can't understand her that's louder. she was never worried about the glass slipper, because her feet are rarely seen in shoes anyway. it's how she connects to the mother she dearly loves and how she lets the wild run without fear of losing a goddamn thing. a smile is all this moonchild needs to be at peace. everything else is just extra that people worry about too much.

stay within the company of
yourself until you are ready
to teach someone how it is
you have become who you
are.

other people will tell you things
about your being, but the soul
of a human knows better than
that.

do not listen to those who talk
about storms as if they are in
love and then become afraid
of the rain.

always dance as if you are in love.

i left this journal here, along with memories, love, and heartbreak, all inscribed in my own way. i didn't know who would find it or how'd they use it if they did. i could go on and tell you how shitty of a hand life has dealt me and how i almost died because i was scared to live, but i enjoy writing about experiences not solely based on my own. i have secrets that don't even know they are secrets. i have told lies just to get out of the simplest of things. i have fallen in love faster than it took me to leave where i was no longer needed because i thought i could salvage the pieces. in doing so, i lost myself to drugs and alcohol and other things people say will kill you. one lesson i've learned in life is once you've experienced death, it still scares you once you've been brought back to life. little things matter to me because they go unnoticed by those not paying attention to who you really are. some are only there to feast on your heart and leave once they have devoured it. leaving the next person who comes along to have what remains. i hope whoever reads this finds closure in some part of their life. we struggle to find words because feelings are needed and we get confused when to use the two. no matter what my record reflects, i am not a failure. i was brave enough to try and it won't be the last time i will pick myself back up. but it will be the last time i trust the person who let me fall.

the doubts you have carried and kept in your heart are not meant to live there forever. it's okay if you're not who people think you are, but being someone you are not for another who you think loves you the same is the quickest way to lose everything.

once communication is severed, life tends to
become fragments of all the things you
once thought were the truth. don't
settle for maybe, when you
deserve absolute
honesty.

the only way to adventure
is to open the wings you've
always had and trust them.
they don't do any good left
at your side. they were
meant to taste the wind
and colors the universe has
given birth to. we attract the
things we believe in and the
stars have been calling your
name. it's time to give them
a visit.

☽

chin up, sweet one, you are someone's most beautiful moment and they might not even know you yet, but they will in due time. you've got that crazy, beautiful, and unforgettable appeal about you. no one ever forgets you and if they do, they aren't sleeping at night. this one time, someone told her to keep walking, and so she walked right into the sun and came out untouched by its flames. she leaves her mark by being kind, but don't get it twisted, she doesn't take shit from anyone. we are all created for certain aspects of life and she was born for greatness. at times, people think she is arrogant because of the way she carries herself, but there's a difference between her confidence and being fake. humans are scared of people like that and always will be. they'll lash out and smother them with negativity because it's what they were taught. but she laughs it off the best she can until she gets home, runs a bubble bath, throws on her pajamas, opens a bottle of wine, and just breathes in the moon before falling back into the dream she had last night about sitting by the ocean and being free from it all, except the wine.

☽

there have been a few times in my life when i thought i was done with finding someone again. years have gone by since the last time i said, "i love you" and meant it. i can't believe how easy it all came together and how you took a heart and put love back into it so effortlessly. my body had been hollowed out by the hands before you and i swore nothing would ever grow again. then all of a sudden life began to sprout in places i didn't know had feelings. my hands started to move with purpose across your legs as you laid them across mine. my eyes refocused on things that mattered and writing turned into novels. my lips craved your taste and it wasn't just a reaction to yours kissing mine.

)

a genuine heart is unstoppable, but sadly it breaks too often on wishes thrown to the sky hoping to be devoured by the universe. the way you trace the outlines of my tattoos makes me believe you can do everything with your eyes closed. you gave me that smile that defeated my fears of not being enough and made me a man.
every time we touch, i am more convinced that we are meant to be together in this lifetime. you are the warm spot on a
brisk autumn day where leaves hope
they fall to feel alive for that brief second before succumbing to the inevitable. you are not my girlfriend or wife, but my soul's voice, and without you, the world would never know the true story of my life.

i've let you love me like no one else.
i've allowed you the ability to do things
to me i'd never let another human ever do.
i've given you the most gruesome parts of
my life and you still love me as if my body
hasn't been ravaged by time and my
carelessness.

i am standing completely naked in front of
you and unashamed of who i am each time
i catch your eyes. i do not ever want to
look into another set and not see us living

out the life we have fought for. if we should
ever blink at anything, let it be between
dreams, where we think we're in another
life without the other.

i have learned over the course of my life that we can fall in love with a variety of moments, places, and things. within each one, we insert people inside of them. regardless of how it unravels or strengthens over time, they sew themselves into our memory. you have already been in my life before, darling. long before memories existed, you and i were alive and in love. i know that by how you've taken over my heart and mind.
you are all four seasons and twelve months which make up my soul's cycle of reason.
we were the words before a language was spoken. we are capable of anything, because we found each other again.

we all get confused about who we should be until the end, and then you wish you could've tried to be yourself for once. don't wait until your next breath is a regret to make a better life for yourself. there's no reason why you can't be happy at this very moment. if you need to do a few things before you get there, conquer them and move forward with what's left. where you are going, love is more important than worrying about what you don't have. confusion is what happens when you forget where you put your feelings, only to remember you left them sitting on the kitchen table for a reason. stay golden and true to yourself, because it's scary out there and people will try their best to make you second guess the silliest of things, including your first name.

)

i had gone so long without laughing i thought living was being silent with the things you love. my eyes had been glued shut by the words you never said and my fingers grew weeds from not being able to touch the life around me. my feet began walking backwards, hoping they left something behind that would advance the day in some weird and exciting way. my soul danced off the end of my tongue; diving into the absence of self. i was less than a human when you left me, but i learned how to admire the shadow of who i was before filling it in with the colors i had given away. my roots are thirsty for something more than just an occasional chance of rain and are too valuable to be left in a drought of intimate confusion. after years of breathing differently, i know that now. if i have learned anything, it is to never let anyone touch your soul with hands washed with uncertainty and to believe in your own magic. if you do those two things, anything is possible.

love is the most sought after form of art there is. copies and multiple prints have been forged and plagiarized to meet the needs of another. art takes patience and practice if you are in search of authenticity. be real with it and don't ever think you can fake out the soul's intuition of another. when you are ready to create, be sure you have accumulated enough days of saying what you mean so that when the time comes for it, someone else will finally believe you.

she is unlike the rest. her life is not measured in moments, but in how many times she laughed at herself when the world thought it had her down for good. there's something natural about her will that guides her through the storms and allows her to be her own sheltering fortress. she's done playing the good one who never questions anything and just goes with the flow of the waves others make. she is a lifetime worth of goodbyes and she's tired of having to be the one who is left without a breath to say hello.

last night, before i went to sleep, my eyes walked back inside of my mind. this week has been stressful, and a passing of a family member compounded it. life has a way of intensifying what matters most when you are feeling more energy than you know what to do with. somehow you learn new ways of coping so you can rest a soul that has stayed out of the body later than expected; trying to play with the universe a little longer. i was remembering images of my great uncle and the times he would say what you couldn't. who would make you laugh just by being himself with the driest of sarcasm spilling out. he was a man who lived his life on his terms and did what he damn well pleased because he wanted to. he was a mountain of a man who made others feel the same. the past couple of years i hardly saw him because he was sick and couldn't make it to my grandmother's house for the holidays. i wish i had one more chance to tell him what he meant to me. i wish i could go back to relive those moments a few more times. my dad's side of the family doesn't cuss that much and when he would drop a few choice words it always made me fold over because of how blunt he was. it's been two days since his passing and last night i was thinking of everything i could and these words came to me: **chaos saved the wild in me**. it saves us all if we are ready to lose our minds on the love beating on the ends of our fingertips. the funeral will be held on monday and i already know my tears will fall, but he would tell me not to. he would call me a name that's frowned upon and i would again laugh one more time with a man who was too much of something else at times to be understood. but i loved that man.

she held a candle to her own hand to finally feel something others could never give to her. all she was asking for was a little more than their best, and yet they walked away in disgust as if giving more than they needed to was going to kill them right there on the spot. when she had a few moments to herself, she took out her heart and placed it in a jar next to the lies.

do we really live in a world where you have to die before you feel something for the first time?

)

even if you aren't meant for me in
this lifetime, the unexpected flavors
and impromptu relationship we have
shared together i'll love regardless of
the future. time can only take away the
human form, not the human spirit.
distance can only separate what others
allow, and we are close to closing the
gap between our crazy and enlivened
hearts. you have invigorated a corpse,
destined for the immortal hands awaiting
me underneath the sea. we will have our
time when we break the glass sun above
us, leaving only the night to welcome
two lovers holding the rest of the sky
together.

being strong is a statement and she wears hers like armor. her walls went up before you and if you find it to be more trouble than it's worth, you know how to leave. people like you do that well and it is the main reason why she continues to build a castle of sanity surrounding a heart in need of protection. she isn't walking around looking for a savior, because she's well equipped to go into battle and defeat anyone or anything trying to break her just for the fun of it. there's no time to waste when you're busy loving and healing yourself after taking multiple knives in the back. there's merit for her actions and not a single

☽

person will tell her otherwise. her scars tell of a great war between her intuition and someone's interpretation of the truth, and she will tell you they are roses waiting to bloom. she lives in thought of one day constructing a new door for others to use, but when countless humans continue to leave things worse than they found them, it's better to shine your own crown. maybe someday she will discover another who is worthy, though when she is honest with herself, the scenery is much more beautiful with dry eyes. she has this smile that can wipe out a city of delusional liars, and she's already used it once before when the wolves came during a full moon.

who you thought you were going to be five, ten, or even twenty years ago might not be who you are today, and you know what, that's okay. we change, evolve, and learn how to love ourselves despite it all. don't let what could have been deter you from what you can do today. the world knows a thing or two about change. it rids itself from things it no longer needs and you are allowed to do the same. perspective is better noticed when you see it for yourself and not from someone who doubts every move you make. learn to appreciate those missed opportunities so you can value a better result for your life. once you do, you will realize the person you were, wants to become so much more than those premature thoughts and ambitions. explore and wander as often as you can. there's a fierce love awaiting you and it might not be with anything specific, but it will be what you need to overcome what you've been through.

☽

you know that spot where it almost killed you.
that spot where you're feeling the most pain.

start there and heal before moving on. if you
do not, it will spread like a wildfire throughout
your bones and all of you will consumed by
self-destruction.

forgive yourself like the stars do when they fall
for empty wishes. even after the pain, they find
a way to shine brighter.

so can you.

)

she rather sleep a little extra in the morning
with the sun coming up. she's not hiding
from anything, because she shows her
true-self when shit needs to get done.

she has grit and it goes well with her
springsteen t-shirt.

she's a top down with the radio turned all
the way up kind of woman. one who could
care less if you don't like her car singing.

it's her concert.

we are born into a world unaware of how terminal life truly is. by the time we finish, we hope there's something beautiful and kind that can take away the thought long enough to honestly enjoy every last drop of freedom resting beneath our feet.

find yours at your own pace, be gentle with yourself along the way, and always appreciate the experience of becoming who you are.

not everyone gets dealt the cards they want, but it's our job to play them the best we can without folding.

it was the simple things that made her fall in love. not so much with a single person, but with the life she had forgot about. nothing cures the aches of loneliness quite like a day to yourself, a strong cup of coffee, and the smell of a sunset coming through an open window. it makes you feel things others cannot provide, and that's how an everlasting connection is created.
by giving your heart a reason to wake up full of belief that something special will happen, you have already won the battle. a fire behind the eyes clears a path you once thought had been lost to the chaos. it was the simple things that made love easy for her to understand, because they were just there for her and she appreciated the gesture of doing something without needing a reason to do so.

☽

i hope to wake up next to you for the rest of my life with my first words being, "i missed you." i want to know how you slept so i can hold you and tell you the morning is more moon than sun because of you. i want to whisper in your ear the flowers of love you've given to me just by being yourself. i want to see you succeed in everything you set your tinker bell heart out to achieve. i want you to find all the things that make your eyes wander and sparkle like the diamonds encrusted in your soul. i want you to be yourself without listening to others who don't think what you are doing is important. they are from a wasteland of prehistoric thoughts and beliefs, and their opinions are dressed as sheep, afraid of being sheared by someone who wears flip

flops or heels. i need you to believe in yourself like i always have and you will find the most important thing in this life is a friendship with your heart. be subtle, but poignant with your decisions. i need you to be by my side when i am in search of a reason why you are still here. i second guess myself and it scares me that it will make you weary and leave. i need you to be my colors because the ones before you, left me gray and my pages wish to feel your hands drawing in the most promising of things.
i cannot wait to wake up next to you and tell you this in person, but for now, i'll let you sleep, because beauty lies within the curves of which you have in the most honest and magical of ways.

she chose herself because others could not see her potential. when people lose sight of their true friends and act out based upon immaturity and selfishness, there's only one person in the wrong. you are responsible for how you behave regardless of how you feel, and her hands were tired of being tied behind her when all she wanted was a group to feel safe with.

you cannot hope for happiness if you yourself are faking who you are. it takes being vulnerable for a few seconds when you swore you'd be swallowed by the madness to feel a sense of meaning. reality is hell for those who are afraid of seeing themselves in the light after the masks come off and i know it's not easy, but what comes next is where you find the strength to take that next step you've always asked your feet to feel. she chose herself not because of a situation, though being shunned by the ones you love is devastating. she had already broke the mold of being fearless so she wasn't trembling at the sound of silence. it was there in the emptiness she finally discovered room for her wings to grow. what an inspiring act it is to be free and rise up as yourself after being told you would never make it. plant doubt all you want, but where there is soul, there is life, and she's dedicated to making it out alive.

tumbling in and out of my chest are words for you. they are clumsy at times, but still find footing in your atmosphere. they come battered, bruised, beaten, and bloodied. they have been formed by a heart and mind that don't always agree, but they're true. it's taken me years to say them, because i needed you to be the one who heard them. i do love you, and loving you has brought me to life when i had been left for dead so many times before. thank you for breathing for me when i had lost my lungs.

)

all i asked for was a chance to be something you never experienced before and you gave me your life without hesitation. sometimes you don't value yourself until you give it away in hopes of it never breaking. you ultimately believe they won't drop you, because they look at you like someone they have never seen before and actually speak to you as if they care. that's all we really want, but some of us go our whole lives without it. instead, we settle for the one who is in bed with us, yet all alone with ourselves. life is nothing more than words being said or kept hidden, and we do our best at trying to explain which ones matter. when you find another who knows everything is important, and not just some things, hold them with all you have.

)

how crazy it all was
to let go and fall
into something
beautiful with eyes
wide open.
amazingly enough,
there's great power
in the release of self,
as you venture out
from the woods
where you thought
you were safe.

☽

if you find yourself at a point in your life where loving someone is no longer what you need, look to decorate your bones with your own happiness. we are only here for a short time and you deserve to be happy no matter the situation you find yourself in. my life had been buried for so long i had no idea which light was mine and the sun would laugh at me for thinking i could burn for as long as he could. it took a few years to get my direction, but i finally figured out that being lost is the only way to live a life too full for even the sky to hold. it has taken me losing all of what i loved to know as long as you have your soul, you are better off than most you see pretending to breathe around you. continue to fill your pockets with adventures and grab as many as you can along the way. life doesn't get easier. it just gets less complicated when you know who you are. be the one who takes a risk and jumps over a few fences to see if the sign was meant to keep you out, or keep you from your dreams. a lot can be learned by not always living by the rules.

never stop opening doors for her and let your eyes walk with hers. never think you have done enough for her, because once you do, you'll think you have achieved something. when in fact, there's only more to give after doing all you can and even then, give your hand to help her when she doesn't ask. she will appreciate kindness in the softest of forms whenever the time calls for it. never stop telling her how the moon is jealous of the way she can hold the light better than anything else you've ever seen. never stop asking her to dance, and when you get the opportunity, surprise her with your love when she least expects it. there's a good chance

☽

her life hasn't been easy, and if it has, then there's no reason to make it difficult with an unreasonable disagreement between your passions. we all have our own way of going about life, but i promise you, it's a hell of a lot easier having someone next to you to lean on from time to time when the weight of reality wants you to be crushed beneath it. never stop telling her how your life is filled with reasons to always be there for her, since she hasn't let you out of her soul since the day you met.

always find beauty in the way her hair falls against her shoulder blades when she removes

)

the day's worries and fears. there's a reason why she is as strong as she looks, and it is not made to be intimidating, only loved for being the lights gathered in the sky for a chance to be understood. love her like the oceans love the melody and you will always hear her in all the places that had gone silent before you met her. don't be afraid to dance with her in the kitchen. it's almost impossible to find a better room than the one you spend the most time in making memories to last. always try and be better at everything you think you're already good at.

practice of self, is worth your energy.

once upon a time, there was a girl who believed love would never find her. during the quiet hours between her thoughts and silence, she discovered herself. maybe she doesn't talk as much as the one next to her. maybe she doesn't smile as much as the one who gets everything. maybe she sleeps with a fire no one sees, because it has a stronger chance at surviving the winters without someone smothering the soul out of it. maybe she's different from you, but don't confuse softness with powerless. even flowers can fight for a patch of sunlight without destroying what they love. pay attention to her kind. she will teach you how being yourself can be the love you've always looked for in those you thought were magic.

☽

it's in the way she wears her baseball cap just

low enough for me to still be able to see her

peaceful eyes. it makes me want to eat her heart

out and taste the freedom in her bones. it drives

me completely crazy, and i love that she knows

it does.

humans will always be flawed, but it's how we choose to love each other that will determine our worth. we are strange and weird creatures looking for those who understand the complexities living inside of us. when we hurt, we do our best to heal ourselves however we see fit. whether it's by drugs, music, solitude, or sex, we all crave something to stop the pain in order to try again where we left off today. life is raw and unscripted. in this world you have to be to get the satisfaction of being alive, or else you are setting yourself up to bleed for something you don't understand and left without closure.

with that in mind, she dared herself to break out
of her comfort zone. up until that point, she had
played it safe with everything, but she knew
if she kept her feet grounded, she'd never
experience the fall. sometimes we must do
the unthinkable to get the one thing that
has escaped us. once you get past your own
security of being shielded, you'll find a heart
stronger than what was holding you back.
so she went on like nothing ever happened
and gave herself a second chance to tickle
the sky with feathers grown from lucid
dreams parading out of her skull.

because of you, i've started to say yes when my mind was telling me to run from everything fear had ever taught me. you are a starting point i never thought i'd arrive at and all of the words i could never type before you. i had gone entirely too long hiding my smile with shame since it isn't perfectly put together. i used to be afraid of who i was, but now i love him because of you. you'll never know how much of an impact you might have on someone until you believe in yourself and the words you say.
be still long enough to know who you are when the world stops moving. it may be the only time

you see what love actually is. sometimes you meet people at an exact moment of life where you thought everything was over, only to realize they are at the same spot, thinking the same thing. i found myself today at a point in my life where peace embraced me and negativity no longer knew where i hurt, because of you. in my personal opinion, the key to life is finding someone who can help us understand our scars and in return, showing them not everyone runs when they speak of heartache.

i'm not sure what she's after, but i know it doesn't matter because she hasn't been stopped yet. when it comes to love, she doesn't want the same as everyone else. her goals are more important than your reasons why it would never work. she's been known to stop people mid-sentence when her time is being wasted. there's a difference between being rude and honest, though you'll probably take offence to her because you've never had anyone ever tell you to be quiet, since your life is that much more important than everyone else's. you will probably mix more drinks than she ever mixes words, but it's best if you stick to what you're good at when being around her. if you're

)

looking for someone to tell you all the good things about yourself and never give you criticism, she's not for you. certain women don't look for crowns to hide behind, because they are too busy fighting battles to worry about someone protecting them. once she figured out how to be the sword instead of the shield, all hell broke loose and let go of its grip. a mindset will only take you as far as you're willing to push yourself. she's not made for everyone. only those who appreciate a woman for her honesty will be able to sit at her table.

there's no more room left for cowards and crows.

i remember studying my mother's face when everyone else was in bed and i was outside with her talking about life. i was too young to understand why faces made certain shapes when pain was painted on them, but i was old enough to know how i felt holding the brush. it wasn't always the things my brothers and i did that caused her to be emotional, though looking back, i'm sure we didn't help matters either. at that age you don't always view things the same as an adult would, even if you knew a broken heart when you saw it. time erases much of who we were and therefore it's forced to sculpt what it can only see. i just wish it would

have been kinder on my soul instead of
carving all the way down to the bone.
there are minuscule nicks made by the
nights i was baptized by the screams that
i now climb up to view to see my mother's
face. the look is the same, but the feelings
have changed, so i continue to climb until
i am eye to eye with who i thought i was;
back when i was a child desperately seeking
love. i didn't know it then, but parents who
you thought loved each other can pretend for
kids, while your mother sits outside studying the
faces of her children, hoping they don't see her
crying. not knowing the blinds show more when
they are down.

i am a darkened forest,
whose trees extend
branches unable
to birth leaves.

illuminate me with
your love and my
roots will forever
be yours.

you are so much more than the things he uses

against you when trying to get under your skin.

don't listen to clowns, love. all they do is walk

around in makeup and tell jokes for kids.

some humans insist on bringing the circus

home with them after work.

☽

sometimes, the bravest thing you can do is get up again when you thought there was nothing left to give. becoming fluent in healing your own brokenness caused by love is the most beautiful thing you can teach yourself. yes, it will hurt and your heart will cry out, but you will overcome it. staying down is what they want you to do, so rise up and defend what's yours.

don't sell yourself short, kid.
being fearless comes at a price
and only accepts the ones with
chaos in their eyes. hold steady
and own whatever you've been
through. someday, someone will
look at you and know it's okay to
keep going.

☽

when you open your
mouth and release the
love you have for
someone, those words,
that breath, turns into
the softest touch you
will ever know in your
life.

)

suffering for the one you love is not love. it's an awful excuse to continue to lose yourself until you are unrecognizable and it's the worst thing that can happen in your life. find your tribe, know who you are, and when you get there, you'll wonder why it took so long before you listened to your intuition. it's the one thing we all have, but don't trust because we are afraid of it being right at times.

i

love

the

way

you

make

my

art

feel.

her favorite flowers are honesty. the ones out in the middle of the field never asking for attention. the ones who are beautiful despite never getting picked.

her bravery came from losing a few petals, but staying forever wild. thrive with conviction and always enjoy the quiet moments you are given.

not everyone loves
silence, but some
crave the freedom
it cultivates.

if i should die,
i hope it's with
your hand in
mine.
if i should live
this life, i hope
it's with your
heart in mine.

)

mismatched socks bring out the best of her. i love when she staggers through the dark in hopes of getting a pair that matches and comes out with my two favorite colors. i love when she snuggles her fears into my heart, knowing they will not last a second longer. i value her strengths and weaknesses, because they make me a better man. be soft with beautiful things and always hold them with two hands. since the first time i could tell the difference between night and day, i knew i was two different people.

☽

seeing her running though the house with these socks on, makes me forget every bad thing that has ever happened in my life. i've found a reciprocating soul who gets me and laughs because we share the silly sides of ourselves with each other, when before they were misunderstood. find a love that always says goodnight to you when you are resting your head on their soft whispers.

☽

we are free to love, yet we stay on branches no longer holding us up to see ourselves. once it breaks, pandemonium ensues and we lose our fucking minds because they told us how it would be, but showed us who they actually are.

not everyone will want the best for you,
and when that person turns into the
keeper of your heart, run. i promise
you it will be frightening, but it will
be the most courageous thing
you will ever do.

keep company with those who find happiness in the simple things and you will see how the ocean speaks of love in each wave it makes for you. there's a reason why the shore never goes lonely during the silence of night.

☽

i picture you in the most innocent and exquisite
of ways. not just sometimes, but in all the time
i've spent wondering if i'd find someone who
could love me in the way i never loved myself.
i have had a lifetime of pain and unforeseen
agony that has left me as alone as the day my
mother gave birth to a son without a name.
i cannot begin to know where to start loving
you the most, because i never knew something
as pure as your soul existed between the
confines of this world and the beating stars

above me. i can only run towards you each time i see you, because the feeling of being without you leaves me fearful of never finding myself again. seeing you as i do now, i understand the cosmos a little more as to why all things are made to be loved and how they are created to be admired and held with a promise of one day having to let go, but being reunited once the chaos stirs up just enough magic for our second act.

when all else seems to fail, be patient with yourself. when you feel you are about to break and no one has your back, be kind to your heart. when you feel completely demoralized and at the bottom of your well, be bold in life with all you have left. do these things so they will understand how you are able to be the best version of yourself when others only saw one side to you. do not get caught up in proving them wrong, just prove to be more than they thought. never think you

)

are too much for someone else. chances are they aren't enough for themselves. there's a reason why you are still here and i can assure you it's not to be less of who you were born to be. make your headlines read what you want them to say. not what others might believe is true. remain your greatest adventure and see how far past the edge of the unknown you are willing to go. you'll find more of what you're looking for out there.

☽

it's both a blessing
and a curse to have
my mind at times.
for when i feel,
it's never the same
twice, and when my
mind is touched by
the universe around
it, the energy
consumes all of
me.

even my love.

maybe forever is
only a shared
breath that
allows your
heart to
finally
beat
with
a
purpose.

)

you will know where to find me

when the day isn't long enough

to tell you just how much you

mean to me.

while we sat in the car, we ate and talked about life for a little over two hours. it was the perfect day and a picnic i could do for the rest of my life.

it's hard knowing that i'll have to leave, but if the universe brought me to you, then i know it will take me back to you when it is our time again to talk about nothing, by doing everything we never could have before.

the unknown is frightening, but it is the main
thing that helps me fight to be with you,
while everyone around me has given up on
their muse and what it takes to find true love
in world dead set on burning everything they
love.

the love between two souls is something the universe conspires with the stars about in order to bring together who has touched its heart the most.

you are i, just as i am you.

we are connected by the desires and dreams shared by the bones of those who could not make it another day without the other they adored. somehow, we have managed to ride the waves and uncertainty, handed out by the moon while experiencing a colossal amount of life. one thing i know for certain, down to the depths of who i am, is our string will never break.

)

and if i am lucky, i will be read by someone who loves me entirely and completely, without ever wanting to put me down. not because what they are reading is any good, but because they feel like holding onto it until the end to see how it all plays out. there's a vulnerable sensation about the way hands can mark pages. the subtle impressions of intent and hope, line the spine of my book, and it is there you will find who i truly am.

in these
empty
sheets
are
where
you can
find my
dreams.

we said, "goodbye" yet we both knew that

tomorrow would begin with a "hello" which

would be the beginning of everything we

once could only talk about.

one day
the sun
will
show its
face,
but until
then, darling,
let's just
dance in
the stars
for now.

it's all about perspective.

we are not what our minds

fear. we are what our hearts

break open for that makes us

fearless in the wild.

the voices repose enough for me at times that i am finally able to understand the thoughts inside of my mind; white noise for the most part, but static electricity nonetheless. it charges me and gives me material so i can allow my soul to vent. it's an adventurous escape. one with fight and purpose. i am thankful for these moments, but they also scare me. so much going on and i feel like i don't have enough time to do them. seems silly to think that, but if you saw the way my words explode when lit by confusion,
you would be scared as well.

all i've ever
been are
bones and
blood.

now those
same things
have found
a way to
become
love.

)

how do you say the words without a witness
to hear you proclaim such a thing?

i brought my heart and left it at your door.

i brought my soul and placed it in the
window of yours.

it's the only way i know how to be in two
places at once.

)

i was made to feel every rotation of the earth
and at times i can barely stand before my feet
forget where they are. i find comfort in the
strange and bizarre we all have trouble
understanding. i am in love with everything
and nothing at once because being bi-polar
you learn to live in-between the shadows and
the light. i remember thinking i'd never live past
thirty, and now i have surpassed that age where
i thought everything would end. most days are
hard for me, because i want more than i have.
i feel like i deserve more than a few scars and
stories to share with people, but then again,
i am thankful for this life. i am not a religious
person and haven't been to church in eight

)

years, even though i know more about the book than those who tell me i am going to hell. i've lied countless times just to get through my day so people would leave me alone. i have a simple life in the fact i wake up, eat breakfast, and then try and write something no one has read before. i make my living off of the stories and ideas lingering in the depths of my mind i had once shut off because of the drugs i took to escape the reality i couldn't stand to be in. my life has been made from mistakes and fate crossing paths when nothing else dared to cross me. in the future i want someone to come home to and go to bed with. you forget how lonely it can get until you go to lay down with emptiness filling the spot next to you and you wonder how

☽

you've made it this far being alone. i miss the cold feet touching mine and the random sex at night when you just need them closer. i miss the way the sounds of someone waking up next to you was the only reason needed to be at peace. someday the connection will find me again, and when it does, all of this will make sense. i am after something many never find, but it's important to me to have it. hopefully in the next thirty years it comes together for me and the life i am in search of, becomes the life i already have. love remains the driving force for all i do. it's what has kept me together all of this time, whether it's been a part of me or not. wherever i am and whoever i am with, just know that love keeps its secrets, but i want to hold you and tell you mine.

☽

i want to be secure and confident in everything i do, but there are times i lose myself to the way the world looks when i close my eyes. i know women want that and you're no different, even though i still feel like i don't deserve you, i do try my best not to let the small things paint who i am. there are days i am okay and think that's enough, but i swear other days make me feel like i have no way of ever keeping you, because it's hard to see what you look at when you think of who i am. we are in constant search of a perfection that doesn't exist, though in our hearts and minds we consistently break a piece of ourselves off when we don't feel like the

☽

other will understand. by the end of it, you wonder why no one appreciates you for the jagged piece of mystery you are. if you aren't comfortable in the place you're standing, no one is going to feel the need to stand next to you when you're sinking back into the hole you call home. i am sorry i feel this way around you, because you are more beautiful than anyone has ever given you credit for being, and i find myself having to prop my soul up against the sky just to keep from falling in front of you. the way you are, makes me realize how fortunate i am for getting past the tragedies i've

been dealt, but still able to attract something so cosmic to a desolate place. i am a shy and awkward human, but i'm hoping it will rid itself of these negative characteristics long enough for me to see i am no different from most.
i am just someone who has a hard time seeing anything good happen to him when so many others need it more.

☽

i know where i came from and always have this feeling of retreating back into the sky to feel some semblance of normalcy. i am not afraid of this place, but i am terrified of the face people see when i try my best to give them an unworthy smile, and i know that they know i am hurting. we're all here to figure out why we are where we are and that's not always what we find before we go. we unearth a profound sense of wanderlust, buried and trapped by flesh and bones. we often retreat because going forward is too easy of a feat for our cold and stubborn feet to move towards. we are incredible humans,

❩

but a few go that way and this way, and we are left scattered amongst the population walking around us trying to see where we fit in. some of us make music, and others take photos of what captures their hearts first. some of us make food too beautiful to eat, and others drive across the country to load and unload cargo not meant for them. some teach us about life, and others teach us about trust and heartache. some take flight to show us anything is possible, and others create technology to help us with our struggle to make it manageable. some just want to roam and be free with no other intention than

becoming closer to what they are afraid of.
they will tell you it's not a life, but if you love
something as much as they love adventure
then you know it's a calling some are just
incapable of understanding because it
doesn't come with instructions. at times
you have to be able to read the universe
inscribed on your heart and learn that it's
okay not to know anything other than
yourself.

)

death stole all of the things i have ever loved.
one thing in particular it took from me was
my sense of just being happy when i
needed to be the most.

the mirror is not only reflection of sadness,
but is colored in confusion as to whether
or not it's telling the truth when it
speaks.

)

there will be days when you can't stand each other and are not on the same page, love her anyway. chances are she knows you better than you know yourself and you have a hard time understanding how that could be, love her anyway. we all could use someone like her and for that reason alone, she's worth it. some of us need to be nudged from time to time by those who know it was the direction we were already going. once you have that, you will embody everything you never thought you were. sometimes, it takes being pushed out of our comfort zone's to see that surviving was the only option we were giving ourselves.

there are so many experiences
that feel rushed nowadays
and it saddens me to see
how many people go
through life
accepting
half
of
everything.

it wasn't her
beauty that
i fell for.

it was in the way her
wings made me feel
like i had my own.

in order to have a good life and one you will want to be a part of, you will have to fight for it. there's no other way around it. tears will be shed, sleepless nights will occur, but one day when you wake up, nothing will hurt and the things you once thought would never go right, will be the reasons why you are no longer worried about the bullshit. we struggle with uncertainty. we are unbalanced at times due to the lack of self-awareness. one thing we all have in common is, we all can create, but have the power to destroy it. be cautious with yourself and love it every chance you get. we forget the most sought after love is our own, and we need to stop depriving ourselves of it.

☽

to the very end we will be us, and with that, you will always be my every dream, every thought, and every reason why i am better today and tomorrow than i was yesterday.
i want to grow old with you. i want to hold your body and feel you move with me every time we make love. i want to kiss your scars and your bruises that you don't think i see.
i want to give you a whole new world so we can explore it together and find the things we love and make it our own. i want to tell you i love you and see the smile on your face and

hear the giggle you make each time our hearts touch. i want you to be happy with things that didn't go right so we can make something better out of them together. you are all the oceans, stars, and mountains living inside the most enchanting and endearing woman i have ever met. and if i'm lucky enough to be able to hold you more times than you've gone without, i will know what it's like to have love in the rarest form.

)

i'm here to tell you that it's okay to hurt and feel pain for people who have left. i'm here to tell you that it's okay to feel everything around you and feel overwhelmed at certain times. i'm here to tell you that anxiety and depression are not diseases, but reality for so many of us. i'm here to tell you that "letting go" does not always mean what you thought, but it won't be the last time you will have to do it. i'm here to tell you all of the things they told you don't mean a goddamn thing because they are exponentially weaker than you. therefore, they chose not to love who you already are. life is a maze in the sense that

)

some stay intent on following the zigs and the zags, while others are simply just there to meet those who want to find a new way out. i'm here to tell you it's okay to be your own sunset while everyone else is worrying about the time. there's a good chance you have been told many things in your lifetime already, and you have let some of it seep into your soul, but you are here to tell others how you became the lighthouse, when you had been a body adrift at sea, screaming for help. i'm here to tell you that you have always been your own rescue call.

i don't always fall in love with myself as often as i should, but within a single blink of an eye, i am love in every place i have yet to touch and feel. buried next to me as i sleep are memories of a time i was in another world with you. maybe one day this sickness will leave me and i will go to hold you and realize i am where this soul is supposed to be. life provides the moments and it is our duty to show up and give it our best effort to make sure we don't miss the ones we were never meant to see in the first place. they aren't hiding. we just become blind to the beauty and forget how easy it is to lose our sight when you've been looking down the whole time, waiting to trip on something worth falling for.

☽

don't be afraid to start over. it can be the hardest thing you do in your life, but if you are willing to welcome the suffering, you will come out of it capable of lifting your heart again in defiance of those who thought the weight of the pain would break you. you are stronger than you think, and if you don't realize it, i hope you read this and feel it for yourself. no matter how many times you thought you've had the soul knocked out of you, it's your choice whether or not you stay down, or get up swinging with the hurricane that's left. i hope you never taste the dirt of where you lay. i hope you never call it home because it feels safe not moving. if there is anything to be afraid of, it's being content dying in the arms of someone who doesn't know what's best for you. the only reason you need to leave is the one you make. the bravest thing you can do is start over. it is then you will discover yourself before they tried to bend you into someone else you never wanted to be. take back your life, take back your smile, and fight every second along the way. whatever you decide to do, don't allow someone to pen an ending to a story if you are still contemplating revising your own. you owe yourself a beautiful life, not an interchangeable lie.

☽

in and out of consciousness i seek
understanding. i am constantly on
the lookout for something more,
something pure from not only
myself, but from those around
me who have a peculiar
madness about them.

**you must seek yourself,
before trying to find
what keeps escaping
you.**

☽

a successful day is me coming home to her and no matter what the universe has thrown at me, it's about making sure she feels the love she deserves. my day isn't complete until her mind and body are both relaxed and comforted.

all of the gifts have been unwrapped and kids are playing with toys santa brought them early this morning. i sit in my chair and look at each one and find such joy and appreciation from the simple things that make us happy.

maybe tomorrow i will get up from this chair and feel differently about the whole damn thing.

chances are i will recline back a bit further and enjoy the presence of being around the ones i love and allow the laughter to keep me from sleeping.

☽

don't go through life afraid of telling someone how much they mean to you. the funny thing is, we are all strangers until we aren't, and it's only then you realize how easy it was and how much time you wasted along the way over-thinking yourself to death. if you love someone, let them know as often as you can. if you need someone's help, reach out to them. i'm sure the person you are nervous to talk to has the same feelings of being rejected. it's not the end of the world if you put yourself out there only to be told, "no." tomorrow eventually comes and if it doesn't, at least you tried. the act alone is courageous and that's what it takes to get what

☽

you want in this society. we are all scared of something, but it shouldn't be talking to another human who you think is immortal and the most beautiful person your eyes have ever witnessed breathing. you have to take a chance when all you've done your entire life is bet against yourself. there's more to you than what you think you see in the mirror telling you to not even attempt what could possibly be the rest of your life. if you don't, someone else will and you'll have to think about it for the next ten or twenty years. there's a lot of wonderful things that can happen in-between now and then, but if you're petrified of saying how you feel

for someone, you're going to shortchange
your own needs. that's when it gets difficult
and monotonous. that's when you die before
your heart has a chance to know what it's like
to feel the wind outside its cage. that's when
you pretend you are living despite the flesh
tearing away from your bones without you
ever noticing or giving a damn. once you
understand that taking a chance is better than
folding the hand you have, which may only be
ace-high, you'll see how you can pull off the
biggest upset by believing you're worth the
blood you have spilled to get to where you
are at today. with or without them, you'll
exceed all expectations you had, because
you jumped without a parachute to feel
the force of it all.

this emptiness inside of me is the lingering air of which i have yet to use accordingly. i have wasted so much needless worry on individuals who never gave a shit about my feelings. when your breath turns into the still and quiet fog resting between your lips and tongue, you need to release it. when you find your breath, make sure it's not just hot air being unleashed into the atmosphere.

come with substance.
come with meaning.
come with fight.

anything less and you're dying a slow death with the purpose inside of you being choked out by the toxicity of humans only looking out for themselves.

☽

don't for a second ever doubt where you are and think to yourself you cannot get through it. we are dreamers. we are fighters. we are lovers. we are brothers. we are daughters. we are fathers. we are mothers. we are superheroes. we are sinners. we are saints. we are the future. we are the eyes and ears of the innocent. we are the hearts searching for reason. we are souls shackled to an idea others try and sell us on. we are the humans preparing for a battle of which we bare the scars from past wars. we are the seekers of everything possible and impossible. we are the fire, shield, and the sword. we are the noise escaping our lungs that cannot hold us in. we are the fists beating our chests when our backs have been pushed beyond their spines. we are the blood spilled that soaks the earth and grows the mountains. we are the tears that fill the cracks and creates the streams the brave drink from. we are the footprints caused by memories of those who could only follow when we needed them to lead. we are eternity, waiting on a moment of insanity to break us. we are the healers and the voodoo of the night.

we are the magic of the stars.

☽

i've come to know that morning doesn't always wake you and it hears more conversations than anyone else you have in your life. it becomes your ally against those who try to take away from you and make you feel as if you are worthless. i've seen my fair share of sunrises and it wasn't always because i wanted to.
i have been in bed, on the ground, in a pair of arms, in my truck, and in a house where i didn't know the people living there. i have been on my

☽

hands and knees next to a toilet, on the tile floor
scared for my life, and in a pasture watching the
fire being smothered by my sorrows and pain.
i have been looking at the sun when it didn't
even know i was staring at it just to feel the
warmth of a shadow who understood me better.
there are these angles in life that just look better
in different places, and when everyone finally
starts to believe in the maps on their hands and
hearts, you will know how connected we all are.

☽

i want to be with you, but i'm scared because i don't know how to make it work. i am at my worst when i allow myself to over-think and manipulate my own heart. "you try and ruin everything because you feel like you don't deserve it." i've been told this so many times over the course of my life. i sit in purgatory as if the universe is telling jokes and i'm the only one who doesn't get it. i feel and connect with the roots of people differently than most. maybe it is sabotage in some weird way, and the truth of it is, i do. how could one person think he deserves so much when all of his life he has never loved himself for who he is? it's my curse, and maybe one day i will feel deserving of the love i have for others and accept that it's okay to feel it in return. i want to be able to believe the

☽

words and feelings others tell me and i have the hardest time doing so because of what's happened to me in the past; back when i believed too much of a good thing will never last. my heart has been made out to be a home for the lonely and i occupy every room in there. i don't make sense to myself most of the time and therefore i ruin every possible thing to make space for more self-loathing. some days when i look into the mirror, i see a reflection that i have no idea how it's standing. maybe down the road we will be able to hold each other and i won't have to worry if i am good enough. i want to promise you so many things, but i know the universe has a way of being unkind to those who continually wish for a better life without putting action behind it. at the end of the day,

☽

i am just a man with a heart that has love to give, but never to himself. tonight and for the past three years i've been in love with someone who i tried to make leave me because i was so scared of not having her, i almost ruined everything we had built so i could find peace in the ruins and have something i feel i belong to. i have been put together differently over the years and i swear each piece has made me better, but i am still attempting to suffer for no other reason than to hurt alone. there's this inescapable sensation i write with and it is the only part of me i truly love. people don't believe me, but he writes to her every night and leaves stars so she won't be alone.

)

i've woken up
several times
thinking i was
still there,
only to see
the sun at a
different angle.

☽

it's not enough to just love you. it seems like my body doesn't respond to anything else but you, and i am a kite caught in a lightning storm when i am around you. the problem is, i don't see myself as others do. all i see is a boy who is still learning how to how to ride his bike on training wheels and waiting on his parents to say "i love you and i am proud of you" one more time as they were before the divorce. i miss those days, but missing them has helped me and saved me from being like them after what they put each other through. though some of their antics spilled into my life and it took me thirty-one years to see its fingerprints

)

on my dreams. i never wanted to drink as a kid because of my mother. i never wanted to be the man my dad was because it wasn't what i thought a man should be. but i looked up to both of them, hoping they'd catch my brothers and i when we were falling in our walk of life.
i turned out to be my mother's child. one who drank when i knew what it would do to me.
it did what i thought it would and almost killed me. i enlisted into the marine corps just as my father did and i have a few stories to tell like he did, but you won't get much more out of me than that. i am a madman looking for an opportunity to be understood and not shoveled aside as if i am a pile of bones

)

without a name. the paradox is, i see myself as someone who deserves absolutely nothing, but wanting everything in the same forgotten breath. it's hard living that way, though i think i have done okay in the pursuit of anything that strikes me as strange and different from the plastic people around me. i am after a meaningful purpose and i will write until i find my path to a place where loving myself is met by your smile. i am sorry for not being more than a boy at times who is frustrated by the handicap he put on his mind. my trust is something i hand out to random people and in return they feel as if they can tell me their story. it's a gift i put in my heart every

☽

day, and because of that, i remain a stranger to this soul of mine. maybe one day i'll know who i am and what it is i am after, but for now, please keep being my friend. i won't always know what to say to you, but i will give you all of my words if you can keep making sense out of them.

to the boy who thought he was a man,
keep falling until you figure out the
balance of life.

☽

you will always be dancing behind my restless eyes, and when i look at everything that is beautiful and free, i will think of you. when these windows of mine close, your silhouette will be a reminder that i lived a life i could be proud of. you are freshly fallen snow on the first day of winter we all want to see once, and the last thing we wish would leave us as the seasons change. you are my favorite color of energy and spontaneity, with a shade of wild behind the halo you wear so gracefully. you are the rain and it will forever have your smell, as it washes over this sin of a man. people talk about being irreplaceable and i know without a single ounce of doubt in my mind that if there ever

☽

were a person, she would laugh like you. we all decide where we go and what we do with our hearts, and i hope tomorrow we can take another step at becoming people who never greet each other as strangers. once you've been touched by the soul of love, you will talk about them with kindness and gratitude for having made such an impact on your life. i thought it was impossible for someone to see me and hold me without falling, because of the weight of my doubts and insecurities, but you stood with it all; brave and ready to carry more than you should have, for me, for us. now it's my turn to take my shoulders and stand beside you as a friend who will never turn his back on the moon that was never in search of a more pristine sky to shine in.

keep beaming with love, sweetheart.

there was a time when i never looked
at walls as an adventure.

that was until i met you and learned how
high you have to go in order to fly over
the ones you were once incapable
of getting over.

☽

before i took this journey, i had to make sure and pack what i needed for a two week trip out at sea. trying to discover something new can be easy. all you have to do is walk out your front door, but i have walked in and out of that damn door too many times now for anything to change. time is a luxury many of us only wear on our wrists or carry with us on our phones for it to amount to anything other than worry. so i am leaving everything here in my safe; locked away in hopes of never needing it again. today is partly cloudy with a chance of regret in the future, though i am confident this outing will provide me new details that can seduce my mind into believing things can get better.
i haven't been gone this long since the birth of my first child and it's something i will always try to find in the things around me. moments we can't get back tend to take away the most from

☽

us and it's why i'm in search of a new place to call my own. a place where pictures don't hang and the wind passes through me like a smooth glass of whiskey. parking my truck, i get out and lock up the last possession i am leaving in hopes of never needing again. starting over saddens me, but there is happiness in my tears only the ocean knows about. i take one last look at where i have called home for twenty-five years, step aboard my boat, put the key in the ignition and ride away from the life of which brought me three children, a wife i will always call a friend, and a story to tell others when i get to where i am going. it's just me and the peace between each wave, and i must say, it's nice to hear nothing and feel everything for the first time in my life.

those

who

dream

of

magic,

will

become

the

stars.

)

you’re the only thing that
makes sense;

like a heart beating for reality,
i need a pulse to escape my
dreams to once and for all
get to you.

☽

when the heart breaks, there's no single part of it that will ever be the same again. as we grow and become who we are, the heart transforms into everything we have loved and lost.

that's why when you give your heart to someone, it takes two people a little bit to figure out how to fit them together.

☽

i lost myself when you
left and now my soul
wanders across the
sands in my chest,
using my bones
to walk.

completely confused
and disoriented,
i lack the
motivation
to
continue.

☽

love and loss are two separate words, yet have

so much in common. with love comes loss and

with loss eventually love grows back in places

you never knew could be alive again.

)

when her wings touched the
sky, she learned how to
become everything
she needed.

a flying smile now streaks
across the horizon's eye.

☽

the eyes feel the heart.
the heart sees the soul.

the soul understands how to laugh just as loud as the moon when it needs to. we often find what we are looking for when we stop searching specifically for that one thing.

all of the answers live within
the flesh we wear.

taste the presence of love in everything you do.
we are still young, and if someone tells you age
describes the bones and not so much the soul,
you need to keep going. there is nothing
substantial there for you to learn.

when the day comes to an
end and the sky is still filled
with stars, you will come
to understand that life
is just a bottle of
hope we all
drink out
of.

even after the last sip is gone.

)

when we unearth the treasures
we have buried deep down inside,
a day becomes a year's worth of
memories.

never take it for granted.
some people are better
thieves than explorers.

we do not always seek the things we truly desire from the fire around us. some of us live in hell, while others are burning alive in their own heaven. i am not sure what's worse:

living while you're dying
or
dying while you're alive.

)

happiness is a great teacher.
even when you cannot stand
to get out of the house
because you are afraid of it
collapsing on you if you leave,
it allows guidance on how to
exit quietly, without disturbing
the foundation.

)

shedding old skin to fit into a world
you don't necessarily believe you
belong to isn't the easiest of things
to do. it's always a mixed bag of
pain and love, but growing is crucial
in this life and you must feel in order
to know how not to when the time
calls for it.

☽

a fresh breath of love
can do wonders for
anyone.

it cleanses the heart
of all the prior
experiences.

each one strengthens
the fight and teaches
us how to let go,

when all we want to do
is hold on as tight as
we can.

)

the only thing she was sure of was the smile she wore. it had taken years to perfect it and the power behind it provided her with the right amount of understanding to know when to use it. life is about trusting ourselves when all else doesn't benefit us anymore. we are the way and the arrow made from the sun to go where we damn well please.

Every so often we
catch a glimpse of
the life we want.

I promise you
if you hold steady,
and true to yourself,
you will be found,
again and again.

Your love is out there.

—Zac ☺

[signature]

CPSIA information can be obtained
at www.ICGtesting.com
Printed in the USA
FFOW03n0135201117
43574345-42350FF